Crisis by Design

The Untold Story of the Global Financial Coup and What You Can Do About It

John Truman Wolfe

Hugo House Publishers, Ltd.

Crisis By Design:
The Untold Story of the Global Financial Coup
and What You Can Do About It

© 2012 by John Truman Wolfe
All rights reserved. Published 2012.

ISBN: 978-1-936449-29-3 (paperback)
Library of Congress Control Number: 2010930683

Hugo House Publishers, Ltd.
Englewood, Colorado
Austin, Texas
877-700-0616
www.HugoHousePublishers.com

Design by NZ Graphics

Praise for *Crisis by Design*

"Wolfe cuts through the smoke and noise and connects some big and ugly dots, documenting his thesis that a cynical international banking cabal has actually engineered one of the greatest global financial squeeze plays yet, in order to extend its already pervasive political, economic, and mental control over the U.S. and other economies and populations. Does such a cynical cabal truly exist? Can the people behind the scenes pulling the strings be truly so selfish and evil? Wolfe mounts a plausible case for an affirmative answer. At the least, readers can get a startling insight into the 'game behind the game,' and how the world of 'the major players' and the shadowy 'kingmakers' might really work. Wolfe pulls no punches and names plenty of names. An eye-opening and educational read."

— Michael Baybak, Financial PR Executive

"Until the true facts of any scene are uncovered and the hidden agendas exposed, the Financial Crisis will continue like the dark clouds over Mordor. The price to pay for such an exposé is astute observation that spans decades. This story can't be understood in a snapshot. The undermining of America, the Freedom she stands for and the U.S. dollar is a scheme that has played out for decades....

"The final question is, Will America have the backbone to rid itself of such repugnant criminals and fix the system before she...? I trust with all my heart the answer is yes. Read the book! Then act!"

— Ned McCrink, Orange County, CA

"Wolfe has done a spectacular job of clearly and logically explaining the real reasons behind our current problems with inflation, the housing crisis, and our economy. His understanding of the subject comes out of thirty years of experience as a financial advisor and one-time banker, and it is this breadth of understanding, coupled with a curious and meticulous mind, that provides the reader with a clear look 'behind the curtain.'"
— Alex Eckelberry, CEO, Sunbelt Software

"John Truman Wolfe is a first-class writer and political commentator who possesses a huge intellect and never ending passion to expose the ills that plague our society. He is an ombudsman for the common man."
— Terry Jastrow, Seven-Time Emmy Award–Winning Producer/Director

"Very few individuals understand the enormity of the subversive and destructive impact on our civilization that originates from the money controllers and manipulators.

"John Truman Wolfe not only understands but has thoroughly documented this situation and identified those responsible. More importantly, he has communicated the data in a way that anyone can understand.

"For anyone desiring financial freedom, the material authored by Wolfe is so vital that it can be truly stated that financial freedom is impossible without a fundamental command of this data.

"That is what Wolfe delivers."
— Larry Byrnes, CEO, Competence Software

"Thank you for the enlightenment. Your laser of truth will penetrate all the lies and expose the truth which we suffer in short supply. You have helped others expand their value as citizens of this great nation."

— Dr. Conrad Maulfair

"You are providing an essential understanding here. We, as 'citizens,' need to understand the increased danger of the age-old game now being played out on a worldwide level— the exploitation by the 'few' of the labor and property of the many. Thank you for a clear view!"

— Glen Wahlquist

"I don't like the idea that our country is so manipulated by the Federal Reserve and their cohorts in the international banking community that our Republic is dying at their whim. Thanks for enlightening us. I hope it will be a wake-up call for our citizens and urge us to take back our country."

— Lloyd McPhee

"I said, Wow!!!!!! I understand now—so much false data that our society puts out creates so much confusion that a person can't act on the situation . . . wondering, and figure-figure, and because they did not have the truth. I now have the truth, and can act and do something about the financial crisis."

— Mary Collins

"Your observations are so refreshing (to the point of chilling) in correctly targeting the key elements and developments! What a bracing antidote to the murky misdirections of the news media."

— Tom Hall, TH Travel

"I was missing the real scene of what the Bank for International Settlements does, and what REALLY happened. You name names. You give a simple chronology of the events leading to our financial woes. You fill in the details that I've never seen. You pulled the cover off an amazing tangle of lies and deceits. I applaud you loudly for your well-thought-out and well-written works."

— Dave Kluge

"John, this is the most PLAUSIBLE explanation I have seen and the most OUTRAGEOUS! You show how and to whom America has been sold out."

— Healy Burnham, D.O., Emergency Physician

"Knowing what has really happened and who did it and why actually empowered more than angered me. Understanding the truth made it easier to move forward!"

— Rick Manning, RM Management Consulting

"Your research regarding the crisis is mind-blowing and eye-opening. It should be taught in business schools all over the globe. If not, the next one is just a matter of time, and it will be much worse."

— Yuval Ivankovski, M.Sc., CEO, Business Diagnosis Institute

"In a world filled with lies and propaganda your writing keeps me connected to the truth that I can sense struggling for breath underneath all the noise."

— Thomas A. Alston, Aero & Marine Tax Professionals

To the Friends of Liberty

TABLE OF CONTENTS

FOREWORD

From the Publisher's Desk —

Throughout America's tumultuous history, there has been a tradition in its literature and letters of compiling essays, articles, pamphlets, etc., into books so that readers could get the sometimes urgent messages in one place and quickly.

Speed was critical because the information these various forms of writing held was vital to the issues at hand—at least that was the conclusion I reached as I sat reading essay after essay, letter after letter, in my apartment in Brooklyn as I worked on my doctorate in English. The similarities were striking: it happened with Alexis de Tocqueville as he traveled throughout New England when the idea of this country was still in its infancy; with Ben Franklin as the Revolutionary War was being fought; with the Federalist *Papers* as the tenets of the Constitution were being debated. It happened with Ralph Waldo Emerson gathering his lectures and essays into books just prior to the Civil War. The list went on and on

These and other eminent American thinkers and writers knew that the great experiment of government representation by its people—and not by some power-hungry dictator—was at stake. They all found themselves at crossroads as the *ideal* of America was being defined, questioned, refined, and, yes, sometimes reformed.

We are, again, at a crossroads in the history of our nation. The current financial crisis that began in 2007 and in which we are digging ourselves ever deeper is causing us to question many of the ideals we hold dear. Our current president is leading us down the path of socialism—a form of government that controls *everything*—not just our healthcare.

More to the point, the "leaders" of our nation have made decisions and signed financial agreements with international financial bodies that may determine the way our very lives are to be handled. They have done this without consulting not only us—the people it most affects—but Congress, the body that is meant to provide oversight in such matters.

These are challenging times for America. We are truly at a watershed moment. Federal budget deficits are beyond being out of control. The government no longer pays attention to the wishes of us, its people, the ones our Founding Fathers fought so hard and so courageously to protect.

We forget that each one of the signers of the Declaration of Independence committed an act of treason against the king of England, punishable by death. One, Thomas McKean of Delaware, wrote John Adams that he was "hunted like a fox by the enemy."[1] He was not alone. They risked everything they held dear to ensure our liberty—our freedom to choose how we live, our right to speak out against our government at any time and for any reason.

That image of a knife through Franklin's throat on the cover isn't just meant to shock, by the way. It's there to help you understand that those in whom we're supposed to trust have instead cut our collective financial throats in order to garner not only gobs and gobs of money but, more insidiously, more power for themselves. Franklin disapproves—just look at his face.

But I digress. In keeping with literary tradition, there has been a deluge of writing about the current catastrophe we're experiencing. Some are more cogent than others. All have helped shed some light on the shadows of what happened with the subprime mortgage scandal. But as I read tract after tract back home in Colorado, I knew there was something missing—connections weren't being made, key information wasn't being presented.

In walks John Truman Wolfe, or rather his essays started appearing in my e-mail inbox. (Franklin would have so loved the Internet, wouldn't he?) From the moment I read his first article, "The Financial Crisis: A Look Behind the

Wizard's Curtain," I knew here was the "something" I was missing. I knew I had to publish this book and *fast*. It contains vitally important information and, like its predecessors in American history, we are sounding the alarm by publishing these clarion calls.

What follows is simply a collection of articles by a person who felt compelled to chronicle the events as he saw them happening. Wolfe wrote each article, documenting an occurrence in the crisis, not knowing that he would be writing the next one. Realizing that some of his readers may not have read the previous article/s, he would often bring some of the prior background information forward to ensure his readers understood the broader context. As you go from article to article, you will witness the story unfold, just as he did—uncovering an agenda by international bankers that is being implemented as I write this.

But Wolfe thoughtfully doesn't just leave us hanging, outraged at what has happened. In the final article, Wolfe provides us with invaluable information on how to preserve our individual financial health. More important, throughout the book he calls for us to act—to make our representative lawmakers stand up to what has happened, to reclaim control of our finances from those who are stripping it away and put it back into the hands in which it belongs—ours.

What you are about to read will incense you—that I promise. But as Wolfe says toward the end, while there has been a coup, "it is not a *fait accompli*." The power-hungry bankers and politicians think they have won—but they haven't, not yet anyway.

This crisis does not just affect our pocketbooks. The very ideal of America—the freedoms and liberties we love and all too often take for granted—are being threatened. It is up to each one of us to speak out, to demand that the right actions be taken, so that this historical moment in American history ends as it has done for the past 230-odd years—on the side of freedom and liberty.

My wish is that you read this book in the spirit in which it was written—hard-hitting, eye-opening, provocative. JTW has a favorite saying, "not on my watch." I hope you adopt it as yours.

Patricia Ross, Ph.D.
June 2010

Postscript: While we have worked to include a glossary of financial terms at the bottom of the pages on which they appear, this book is full of such. I urge you to use a dictionary liberally. Look up words you don't understand. As Noah Webster, creator of the first American Dictionary said, "There is one remarkable circumstance in our own history which seems to have escaped observation—the mischievous (causing damage) effect of the indefinite application of terms. . . . Popular errors proceeding from a misunderstanding of words are among the...cause of our political disorders."[2] We have enough "political disorder" right now—don't compound it by not understanding the words you read!

INTRODUCTION

I never wanted to be a banker.

In graduate school, I was captivated by the study of nineteenth-century American history—the era when the promise of free and unexplored land pulled the young Republic ever westward to the golden coast. It was the mystery and promise of what was over the next mountain that drew us across the most glorious land imaginable.

So I resisted when my father visited me as I was wrapping up my master's degree and asked, in the most humble manner I had ever heard him speak, if I would drop my plans for a Ph.D. at Berkeley and take over the family home furnishing business—a retail store that was one of the most prominent in the San Francisco Bay Area.

Let me state the problem in the simplest possible terms: the young academic liberal confronting a life as a card-carrying member of the bourgeoisie. Dear God.

So you may be surprised to hear that, after some consideration, I said, "Yes." I said yes for two reasons, neither of which I would recommend as the basis for a happy life.

I felt I owed it to him. I was the oldest son and my two brothers were not interested. How could I let my dad spend his life building a business and not provide a way to let him retire and enjoy his "old age"?

And then there was the financial factor. I was twenty three, had been married two years, and had a one-year-old daughter. I had been living on the proverbial graduate student rations of beans and rice, and I was tired of it. The oh-so-capitalist vision of earning a fat paycheck as the heir apparent to a successful Bay Area furniture brand and playing a lot of golf turned me into a materialist faster than you can say "family country club membership."

It took a few years and some unaccustomed soul searching to wake up to the fact that neither of these motivations aligned with my basic purpose in life, which was to research and write.

The glories of Joseph Walker's trek across the southern Sierra Nevada in the 1830s and selling blue-collar suburbanites the new twenty-three-inch Motorola color TV for 10 percent down and twenty-four equal monthly payments did not fit in the same universe. I taught American history at night down at Oakland Technical High School, the birthplace of the Black Panther Party. This certified me as a gold-seal liberal, but it wasn't enough, and after a few years I left and went looking for a full-time teaching job.

After a month of flogging résumés to college administrators who appeared to have been dining on the mind-bending menu of Haight-Ashbury for the previous several years, the family bank account was running on fumes and was beginning to sputter. It was at that point that a friend of a friend told me that Security National Bank—a local retail banking chain—was looking for loan officers.

At this juncture I would have considered a job as a hairdresser in San Francisco, so I rushed down to the bank's headquarters for an interview.

Some may be surprised to learn that the study of the westward movement of the American frontier does not teach one about banking. But working for my dad had done just that. As the assistant controller and credit manager, I dealt with banks and the financing of consumer goods on a daily basis. Additionally, I was under the tutelage of the company's fastidiously demanding controller, who insisted that I balance the company's books literally to the penny every month. So I learned bookkeeping, accounting, and financial statements as a matter of hands-on practice. And so I came to the bank with an understanding of credit and finance and the always coveted graduate degree. Even though it was entirely off the subject, it presumably was evidence that my IQ was above roadkill.

Besides, management at SNB were all UC Berkeley guys, and while my degree came from San Jose State, I had done extensive research for my thesis at The Bancroft Library. Situated on the Berkeley campus, Bancroft is one of the finest repositories of Western Americana in the world. So, although I wasn't a full blood brother, I had hunted on the tribe's sacred grounds.

I was hired on the spot.

For reasons that remain unclear to me to this day, I took an instant liking to banking and stormed up the corporate ladder as if someone had slapped a turbocharger on my career. But my point in all of this is that it was here, immersed in the world of Bay Area banking, that I began using my graduate school research chops to explore the broader subjects of global credit markets, investments, and the oh-so-mysterious universe of the organs of international finance.

PR Spin: How to Move Financial Markets

There were two books that I credit with turning a naïve young banker, a virgin to the world of Wall Street corruption, into a budding financial sleuth.

The first was a book called *The Wall Street Gang*, written by a successful Los Angeles–based money manager named Richard Ney. The text lays bare how "specialists"— those who handle the buy and sell orders of major stocks*—manipulated and controlled the New York Stock Exchange.[1]

The other, with the corny-sounding title of *How to Make the Stock Market Make Money for You*, was written by a man named Ted Warren.[2] Warren uses long-term graphs that show the manipulation of virtually all major stocks and most of the commodities.[†]

I didn't take the data in these publications for granted. I tested the theories again and again. Warren's strategies, spelled out in clear, everyday English, worked then and still work today.

More to the point of this introduction, these books provided clear evidence that the major investment markets—stocks and commodities in particular—are controlled. Period.

This, at the time, was a revelation, which has served me well in the ensuing years. Despite well-ingrained illusions to the contrary, things do not just happen in the world of investment and finance. They are caused. Orchestrated by forces unseen by the general public, sophisticated public-relations campaigns are rolled out via well-connected media networks to spin the strategic messages that flank the campaign *du jour*.

---

*Stock(s)—Short for stock certificate. A document representing the number of shares of a corporation owned by a shareholder.

†Commodities—A commodity is food, metal, or another fixed physical substance that investors buy or sell. For example, corn, gold, currency such

Once I understood that the actions of the investing public were shaped by financial PR machines, I began reading the press with that perspective. In other words, I looked for the underlying intention of the article— what it was trying to get people to do as opposed to the surface message.

It wasn't hard to see this at work. Some years ago, I was following a particular commodity, which appeared to be under accumulation by forces that I felt would drive the price higher. I bought some.

Weeks later, an article appeared in the *Wall Street Journal* saying that an international organization that was in charge of setting the price for this commodity had agreed that the price was not going to exceed a certain level for the foreseeable future. This was just a few cents higher than what I had paid.

The chart of the commodity demonstrated that it was under accumulation by someone/s. My assessment was that they were trying to scare people away from the commodity so they could buy more.

I bought some more—as did, I'm sure, the insiders.

Shortly thereafter, the price of the commodity started to rise. I kept buying as the price went up and the news remained negative or neutral. Several months later, about the time it had tripled, a positive article about the commodity appeared in the *Wall Street Journal*.

Over the next ten days, three more articles appeared in the financial press promoting it as a good investment.

My take now was that the insiders were seeking to increase the number of people buying the commodity so they could sell theirs.

I called my broker. I asked him what his firm's stance was on the commodity. "They just issued a 'buy order'"—meaning they were telling their brokers to recommend it to clients.

"Sell," I said. "All contracts."

The price went up for another few days and then crashed.

Articles in the financial press that promote the buying or selling of an investment product are often not news, but PR spin written with an intention to covertly mold the public's behavior about the investment. This is not an invariable rule, but if you read stories that seem to aggressively promote a particular investment (either positively or negatively) in the mainstream financial media, follow the results into the future. You will often find that the prediction not only missed, but the opposite occurred. Try it.

To be sure, there are exceptions. But these are often young start-up companies that are not traded on major exchanges.

Sometimes the negative PR campaign is designed to take the player all the way out, *à la* Lehman Brothers on September 15, 2008, as opposed to driving the price down so it can be purchased for pennies on the dollar, *à la* Washington Mutual ten days later.

If you read the books referenced above and start following these things in the media, you'll get sharp at this.

The IMF and the World Bank

This perspective was extremely helpful to me when I started following the activities of the World Bank and the International Monetary Fund (IMF). These are "sister" organizations that were set up at the end of the Second World War essentially to help rebuild war-torn Europe with low-cost loans (the World Bank) and to foster stability in the international currency markets (the IMF).

Despite their altruistic-sounding charters, these two organizations have become nothing less than global financial predators that have turned three-fourths of the planet into debt-ridden junkies.[3]

Sometimes evil is hard to confront. But I tell you without equivocation that the activities of these two international banks have been motivated by a cold, calculated plan to control the populations of Earth.

I know, I know—conspiracy theory and all that. But if you study their trail of financial bondage across the planet, their real intentions become all too clear. And it is not a matter of studying their conduct for a year or two; their strategic plans started decades in the past and run decades into the future.

I started monitoring their activities while working for Security National in the mid-seventies. Some years later, I followed a major currency crisis in Mexico. I found it odd that the IMF had moved in with a multibillion-dollar "saving" loan. At first, I was interested from a banker's perspective. What had they taken as collateral? I mean, what does an international bank take as security for a loan: oil refineries, mines, government lands? What?

Somehow I got hold of the loan agreement between the IMF and Mexico—a James Bond moment—and I read it. Some of the provisions appeared to have been written by Orwell himself. They granted the IMF control over a wide range of social policies, many of which had no bearing on Mexico's ability to repay the loan.

Something was very odd in the land of many bankers.

It was at that point that I started following the activities of the IMF and World Bank more closely as they engaged in an international crime spree that spread economic terrorism around the planet like a fiscal virus.

Having tracked them now for more than three decades, I can tell you that their pattern of operation repeats itself, country to country.

First, they covertly facilitate a currency crisis in the targeted country. This is not difficult to do if one understands that currencies are commodities and can be manipulated on the exchanges on which they trade. It takes capital to do it, but the mechanics are not difficult to put in place. In recent years, people like George Soros have been involved. Think Indonesia, late nineties. Soros and well-placed media outlets push the message about how weak the targeted currency is. Because of this, he is able to sell the currency short* ("betting" it will go down). In this way he drives the value of the currency even lower while making a killing. As the currency crashes, the country experiences growing economic chaos, riots, and internal strife.[4]

With the country now trying to participate in international trade and commerce using a currency that has all the attraction of pet food from China, their credit rating nose-dives faster than a Nancy Pelosi popularity poll. They can't borrow from traditional sources. Business falters. Unemployment skyrockets. And in some cases, again like Indonesia, riots ensue and blood flows. When the politicians have their colons sufficiently puckered,

---

*Sell short—You think a stock/commodity will go down in price. Your broker allows you to borrow these shares of stock. He then sells them at today's high price. You agree to buy them back at a lower price. When the stock goes down to your preset lower price, you buy them back. You pocket the difference. You lose if the value of the stock goes up.

one or both of the twin sisters of the Apocalypse (the IMF and World Bank) ride in on a white horse.

"Gee, Mr. President. It looks like you're having a problem here. Perhaps we can provide some assistance. Would, say, five or ten billion help to tide you over?"

"Yes, well, the New York bankers have turned their backs on us for no reason at all. This currency issue is temporary, I assure you. How much did you say?"

"Five or ten billion, but we're flexible. Our concern is for the people of your great nation."

"Yes, of course. Who controls how the money is spent?"

"You do, sir."

The president suppresses a smile as he thinks of his private yacht moored in the south of France and his young mistress sunbathing on the foredeck in her topless bikini.

"And what would the terms be?"

"Interest only for the first three years and then we would work out a mutually agreeable repayment plan for the principal. And, of course, you would have to execute our standard loan agreement."

"Certainly. Do you have a copy of that handy?"

One of the bankers pulls a multipage document out of a Gucci briefcase of shimmering Italian leather and hands it to the president. He begins to scan through it. His brow furrows. He looks up.

"Eh . . . why is there a clause here that mandates how we must educate our young women on matters of family planning and contraception? That has nothing to do with the country's economic strength."

"Well, Mr. President, we feel it does. The population level of the country certainly has a bearing on the nation's prosperity. Wouldn't you agree?"

"I . . . eh, suppose so. But I can't agree to these stipulations regarding our agricultural production or our tax policies. Those are strictly internal matters." The president stands and straightens his back.

The two bankers stand as well. "We're sorry to hear that, Mr. President. We were hoping we could help you reduce those unemployment figures." They head for the door. One of them turns, "And Marseille is . . . so beautiful this time of year."

Two weeks later headlines blare: *President Signs $10 Billion IMF Loan Agreement.*

The president puts a cool $500 million in his Swiss bank account. A frenzied pack of federal bureaucrats feast on the balance until only the remains of the bloodied carcass are left for state and local vultures. Perhaps 10 percent will reach the people.

The country will never be able to repay the loan, which, of course, is exactly what the IMF wanted in the first place—control of the country's assets and the ability to dictate social engineering policy.

I know—you think that's a fairy story, an allegory, a fable.

But I have watched this scenario roll out from Moscow to Mexico, from Seoul to Jakarta, for more than thirty years now and this is the drill. The mistress and the dialogue are of course touches of fiction, but the externally *created* currency crisis, economic turmoil, the white horse, the "saving" loan with the Orwellian loan agreements, have been the essence of international banking since the 1970s and perhaps earlier.[5]

Alarm Bells—the GMA

I wrote an article about this in the late nineties but had left the subject alone from a literary perspective since then. It was a statement by the president of the New York Federal Reserve Bank in March 2008 calling for a GMA—a Global Monetary Authority—that set off the alarm bells anew.

A GMA is essentially a planetary financial dictator.

And as you likely know, the president of the New York Fed* at that time was none other than Timothy "Pretty Boy" Geithner, the current U.S. Treasury secretary. So I

---

*New York Fed—New York branch of the Federal Reserve Bank.

started a new round of research and writing. Over the next year and a half, I wrote several articles about not only what had happened but, of greater concern, why. They comprise the main body of this book.

You see, this financial crisis was and is a *crisis by design.* And there has been a *coup d'état*—a hostile takeover—of our financial systems. In order to do anything about it, you first need to know how and why it happened. That is the story of this book.

One of the things that I found in my recent research is that there is an organization behind the IMF and World Bank that is calling the shots, which turns out to be the key puppeteer. Exposing that entity, as well as what you can do about this personally to protect yourself and what we need to do as a matter of public policy, is the basis of this book.

I hope you enjoy the read. More importantly, I hope the book helps raise your awareness and empowers you to act.

John Truman Wolfe
November 2009

1

The Financial Crisis:
A Look Behind the Wizard's Curtain

March 2009

I'm tired of hearing about *subprime* mortgages.*

It's as if these things were living entities that had spawned an epidemic of economic pornography.

Subprime mortgages are as much a cause of the current financial chaos as bullets were for the death of JFK.

Someone planned the assassination and someone pulled the trigger.

The media, J. Edgar Hoover, and the Warren Commission tried to push Lee Harvey Oswald off on the American public. They didn't buy it.

They shouldn't buy subprime mortgages either.

Someone planned the assassination and someone pulled the trigger. Only this time the target is the international financial structure and the bullets are still being fired.

---

*Subprime—Nonprime or second-chance lending. Borrowers with some late payments or poor credit will get higher interest rates than those for prime borrowers.

Oh yes, people took out adjustable-rate mortgages they could ill afford, which were then sold to Wall Street bankers. The bankers bundled them up like gift wrappers at Nordstrom during the holidays and sold them to other banks after raking off billions in fees. The fees? They were for . . . well . . . they were for wrapping the mortgages in the haute couture of Wall Street.

But it didn't start there. No, no, not by a long shot.

So, as the late, great Paul Harvey would say, "And now you're going to hear the *rest of the story.*"[1]

Are subprime mortgages part of some larger agenda?

And if so, what is it?

Stay with me here because Alice is about to slide down the rabbit hole into the looking-glass world of international finance.

Easy Money Alan

There are various places we could start this story, but we will begin with the 1987 ascendancy of Rockefeller/ Rothschild homeboy Alan Greenspan from the board of directors of J.P. Morgan to the throne of chairman of the Federal Reserve Bank (a position he was to hold for twenty years).

From the beginning of his term as chair, Greenspan was a strong advocate for deregulating the financial services industry: letting the cowboys of Wall Street sow their wild financial oats, so to speak.

He also kept interest rates artificially low, as if he had sprayed the boardroom of the Federal Reserve Bank with some kind of fiscal aspartame.[2]

While aspartame (an artificial sweetener branded as Equal and NutraSweet) keeps the calories down, it has this itty-bitty side effect of converting to formaldehyde in the human body and creating brain lesions.

As we are dealing here with a gruesomely tortured metaphor, let me explain: I am not suggesting that Chairman Greenspan put Equal in his morning coffee, but rather that by his direct influence, interest rates were forced artificially low resulting in an orgy of borrowing and toxic side effects for the entire economy.

The Community Reinvestment Act

Greenspan had been the Fed chairman for seven years when, in 1994, a bill called the Community Reinvestment Act (CRA) was rewritten by Congress. The new version had the purpose of providing loans to help deserving minorities afford homes. Nice thought, but the new legislation opened the door to loans that set aside certain lending criteria: little things like a down payment, enough income to service the mortgage, and a good credit record.[3]

With CRA's facelift, we have in place two of the five elements of the perfect financial storm: Alan "Easy Money" Greenspan at the helm of the Fed and a piece of legislation that turned mortgage lenders into a division of the Salvation Army.

Perhaps you can see the pot beginning to boil here. But the real fuel to the fire was yet to come.

Glass-Steagall

To understand the third element of the storm, we travel back in time to the Great Depression and the 1933 passage of a federal law called the Glass-Steagall Act. As excess speculation by banks was one of the key factors of the banking collapse of 1929, this law forbade commercial banks from underwriting—in other words promoting and selling—stocks and bonds.[4]

That activity was left to the purview of "investment banks" (names of major investment banks you might recognize include Goldman Sachs, Morgan Stanley, and the recently deceased Lehman Brothers).

Commercial banks could take deposits and make loans to people.

Investment banks underwrote stocks and bonds.*

---

*Investment banks look over a company and then decide to promote the stock; they do due diligence first, of course, but "underwriting" is more of a sales game than anything.

To repeat, this law was put in place to prevent the banking speculation that caused the Great Depression. Among other regulations, Glass-Steagall kept commercial banks out of securities.*[5]

Greenspan's role in our not-so-little drama is made clear in one of his first speeches before Congress in 1987 in which he calls for the repeal of the Glass-Steagall Act. In other words, he's trying to get rid of the legislation that kept a lid on banks speculating in financial markets with securities.

He continued to push for the repeal until 1999 when New York banks successfully lobbied Congress to repeal the Glass-Steagall Act. Easy Money Alan hailed the repeal as a revolution in finance.[6]

Yeah, baby!

A revolution was coming.

With Glass-Steagall gone, and the permissible mergers of commercial banks with investment banks, there was nothing to prevent these combined financial institutions from packaging up the subprime CRA mortgages with normal prime loans and selling them off as mortgage-backed securities through a different arm of the same financial institution. No external due diligence required.[7]

---

*Securities—Certificates of creditorship or property carrying the right to receive interest or dividend, such as shares or bonds.

You now have three of the five Horsemen of the Fiscal Apocalypse: Greenspan, CRA mortgages, and repeal of Glass-Steagall.

Waiver of Capital Requirements

Enter Hammering Hank Paulson.

In April of 2004, a group of five investment banks met with the regulators at the Securities and Exchange Commission (SEC) and convinced them to waive a rule that required the banks to maintain a certain level of reserves.

This freed up an enormous reservoir of capital, which the investment banks were able to use to purchase oceans of mortgage-backed securities (cleverly spiked with the subprime CRA loans like a martini in a Bond movie). The banks kept some of these packages for their own portfolios but also sold them by the bucketload to willing buyers from every corner of the globe.

The investment bank that took the lead in getting the SEC to waive the minimum reserve regulation was Goldman Sachs. The person responsible for securing the waiver was Goldman's chairman, a man named Henry Paulson.[8]

With the reserve rule now removed, Paulson became Wall Street's most aggressive player, leveraging the relaxed regulatory environment into a sales and marketing jihad of mortgage-backed securities and similar instruments.

Goldman made billions. And Hammering Hank? According to *Forbes* magazine, his partnership interest in Goldman in 2006 was worth $632 million. This on top of his $15 million per year in annual compensation.[9] Despite his glistening dome, let's say Hank was having a good hair day.

In case this isn't clear, it was Paulson who, more than anyone else on Wall Street, was responsible for the boom in selling the toxic mortgage-backed securities to anyone who could write a check.

Many of you may recognize the name Hank Paulson. It was Paulson who left the Goldman Sachs chairmanship and came to Washington in mid-2006 as George Bush's secretary of the Treasury.

And it was Paulson who bludgeoned Congress out of $700 billion of so-called stimulus money with threats of public riots and financial Armageddon if they did not cough up the dough. He then used $300 billion to "bail out" his Wall Street homeboys to whom he had sold the toxic paper in the first place.[10] All at taxpayer expense.

Makes you feel warm all over, doesn't it?

Congress has its own responsibility for this fiscal madness, but that's another story.

This one still has one more piece—the *pièce de résistance*.

Basel II and the Bank for International Settlements

Greenspan, the Community Reinvestment Act, the repeal of Glass-Steagall, and Paulson getting the SEC to waive the capital rule for investment banks have all set the stage: the economy is screaming along, real estate is in a decade-long boom, and the stock market is reaching new highs. Paychecks are fat.

But by the first quarter of 2007, the first nigglings that all was not well in the land of the mortgage-backed securities began to filter into the press. And like a chill whisper rustling through the forest, mentions of rising delinquencies and foreclosures began to be heard.[11]

Still, the stock market continued to rise, with the Dow Jones reaching a high of 14,164 on October 9, 2007. It stayed in the 13,000 range through the month, but in November, a major stock market crash commenced from which we have yet to recover.[12]

It's not just the U.S. stock market that has crashed, however. Stock exchanges around the world have fallen like a rock off a tall building. Most have lost half their value, wiping out countless trillions.[13]

If it were just stock markets, that would be bad enough. But let's be frank; the entire financial structure of the planet has gone into a tailspin and it has yet to hit ground zero.

While there surely would have been losses, truth be told, the U.S. banking system would likely have gotten through this, as would have the rest of the world, had it not been for an *accounting rule* called Basel II promulgated by the Bank for International Settlements.

Who? What?

That's right, I said an accounting rule.

The final nail in the coffin—and this was really the wooden spike through the heart of the financial markets— was delivered in Basel, Switzerland, at the Bank for International Settlements.

Never heard of it? Neither have most people; so, let me pull back the wizard's curtain.

Central banks are privately owned financial institutions that govern a country's monetary policy and create that country's money.

The Bank for International Settlements (BIS), located in Basel, Switzerland, is the central bankers' bank. There are fifty-five central banks around the planet that are members, but the BIS is controlled by a board of directors, which is comprised of the elite central bankers of eleven different countries (U.S., UK, Belgium, Canada, France, Germany, Italy, Japan, Switzerland, the Netherlands, and Sweden).

Created in 1930, the BIS is owned by its member central banks, which, again, are private entities. The

buildings and surroundings that are used for the purpose
of the bank are inviolable. No agent of the Swiss public
authorities may enter the premises without the express
consent of the bank. The bank exercises supervision
and police power over its premises. The bank enjoys
immunity from criminal and administrative jurisdiction.

In short, they are above the law.

This is the ultrasecret world of the planet's central
bankers and the top of the food chain in international
finance. The board members fly into Switzerland for
once-a-month meetings, which they hold in secret.

In 1988 the BIS issued a set of recommendations on
how much capital commercial banks should have. This
standard, referred to as Basel I, was adopted worldwide.

In January of 2004 our boys got together again and
issued new rules about the capitalization of banks (for those
that are not fluent in bank-speak, this is essentially what the
bank has in reserves to protect itself and its depositors).

This was called Basel II.

Within Basel II was an accounting rule that required
banks to adjust the value of their marketable securities
(such as mortgage-backed securities) to the "market price"
of the security. This is called *mark to market*. There can
be some rationality to this in certain circumstances, but
here's what happened.

The Media and Mark to Market

As news and rumors began to circulate about some of the subprime CRA loans in the packages of mortgage-backed securities, the press, always at the ready to forward the most salacious and destructive information available, started promoting these problems.[14]

As a result, the value of these securities fell. And when one particular bank did seek to sell some of these securities, they got bargain-basement prices.

Instantly, per Basel II, that meant that the hundreds of billions of dollars of these securities being held by banks around the world had to be marked down—*marked to the market*.[15]

It didn't matter that the vast majority of the loans (90 percent plus) in these portfolios were paying on time.[16] If, say, Lehman Brothers had gotten fire-sale prices for their mortgage-backed securities, the other banks, which held these assets on their books, now had to mark to market, driving *their* financial statements into the toilet.

Again, it didn't matter that the banks were receiving payments (cash flow) from their loan portfolios; the value of the package of loans had to be written down.

A rough example would be if the houses on your street were all worth about $400,000. You owe $300,000 on your place and so have $100,000 in equity. Your neighbor, Bill, in selling his house, uncovered a massive invasion of termites. He had to sell the house in a hurry and wound up with $200,000, half the real value.

Shortly thereafter, you get a demand letter from your bank for $100,000 because your house is only worth $200,000 according to "the market." Your house doesn't have termites, or perhaps just a few. Doesn't matter.

Of course, if the value of your home goes below the loan value, banks can't make you cough up the difference.

But if you are a bank, Basel II says you must adjust the value of your mortgage-backed securities if another bank sold for less—termites or no.

When the value of their assets was marked down, it dramatically reduced their capital (reserves), and this—*their capital—determined the amount of loans they could make.*

The result? Banks couldn't lend. The credit markets froze.

Someone recently said that credit was the *life blood* of the economy.[17]

This happens to be a lie. Hard work, production, and the creation of products that are needed and wanted by others—these are the true life blood of an economy.

But let's be honest; credit does drive much of the current U.S. economy: home mortgages, auto loans, and Visas in more flavors than a Baskin-Robbins store.

That is, until the banks had to mark to market and turn the IV off.

The Crisis

With mark to market, mortgage lending slammed to a halt as if it had run headlong into a cement wall, credit lines were canceled, and credit card limits were reduced and in some cases eliminated altogether.[18] In short, with their balance sheets butchered by Basel II, banks were themselves going under and those that weren't simply stopped lending. The results were like something from a financial horror film—if there were such a thing.

Prof. Peter Spencer, one of Britain's leading economists, makes it very clear that the Basel II regulations ". . . are the root cause of the crunch . . ." and that "if . . . the authorities retain the strict Basel regulations, the full scale of the eventual credit crunch and economic slump could be 'disastrous.'"

"The consequences for the macro-economy," he says, "of not relaxing [the Basel regulations] are unthinkable."[19]

Spencer isn't the only one who sees this. There have been calls in both the U.S. and abroad to, at least, relax Basel II until the crisis is over. But the Boys from Basel haven't budged an inch. The U.S. did modify these rules somewhat a year after the devastation had taken place here, but the rules are still fully in place in the rest of the world and the results are appalling.

The credit crisis that started in the U.S. has spread around the globe with the speed that only the digital universe could make possible. You'd think Mr. Freeze from the 1997 *Batman & Robin* movie was doing his thing.

We have already noted that stock markets around the world have lost half of their value, erasing trillions. Some selected planet-wide stats make it clear that it is not just stock values that have crashed.

As of this writing, China's industrial production fell 12 percent last year, while Japan's exports to China fell 45 percent and Taiwan's were off 55 percent. South Korea's overseas shipments decreased 17 percent, while their economy shrank 5.6 percent.

Singapore's exports were off the most in thirty-three years and Hong Kong's exports plunged the most in fifty years.

Germany had a 7.3 percent decline in exports in the fourth quarter of last year, while Great Britain's real estate market declined 18 percent in the last quarter compared to a year earlier.

Australia's manufacturing contracted at a record pace last month, bringing the index to the lowest level on record.[20]

There's much more, but I think it is obvious that the "credit pipe" can no longer be smoked.

Welcome to planetary cold turkey.

Oddities

It is fascinating to look at the date coincidence of the crash in the U.S. Earlier I noted that the stock market continued to rise throughout 2007, peaking in October of 2007. The dip in October turned to a rout in November.

The Basel II standards were implemented here by the U.S. Financial Accounting Standards on November 15, 2007.

There are more oddities.

Despite the fact that Hammering Hank dished out hundreds of billions to his banker buddies to "stimulate" the economy and defrost the credit markets, the recipients of these taxpayer bailout billions have made it clear that they will be *reducing* the amount of money they will be lending over the next eighteen months by as much as $2 trillion to conform to Basel II.

What do you think—Hank, with his Harvard MBA, didn't know? The former chairman of the most success-ful investment bank in the world didn't know that the Basel II regulations would inhibit his homies from turning the lending back on?

Maybe it slipped his mind.

Like the provision he put into his magnum opus, the $700 billion bailout called TARP. It carried a provision for the Federal Reserve to start paying interest on the money banks deposited with it.[21]

Think this through for a minute. The apparent problem is that the credit markets are frozen. Banks aren't lending. They can't use the money from TARP to lend because Basel II says they can't. On top of this, Paulson's bailout lets the Fed pay interest on funds banks deposit there.

If I am the president of a bank, and let's say that I'm not Basel II impaired, why in the world am I going to lend to customers in the midst of the worst financial crisis in human history when I can click a mouse and deposit my funds with the Fed and sit back and earn interest from them until the chaos subsides?

But, hey, maybe Hank's been putting aspartame in his coffee.

No, this stuff is as obvious as the neon signs on Broadway to the folks who play this game. This is banking 101.

So, given the provisions of Basel II and the refusal of the BIS to lift or suspend the regulations when they are clearly the driving force behind the planet-wide credit crisis, and considering the lack of provisions in Paulson's bailout bill to mandate that taxpayer funds given to banks must actually be lent, and given the added incentive in the bill for banks to deposit their bread with the Fed, one gets the idea that maybe, just maybe, these programs weren't designed to cure this crisis; maybe they were designed to create it.

Indeed, my friends, this is crisis by design.

Someone planned the assassination, and someone pulled the trigger.

The Rubber Meets the Road

All of which begs the question, how come?

Why drive the planet into the throes of fiscal withdrawal—of job losses, vaporized home equity, and pillaged 401(k)s and IRAs?*

Because when the pain is bad enough, when the stock markets are in shambles, when the cities are teaming with the unemployed, when the streets are awash with riots, when governments are drenched in the sweat of eviction and overthrow, then the doctor will come with the needle of International Financial Control.

This string of ineffective solutions put forth by people who know better are convincing bankers, investors, corporations, and governments of one thing: the system

---

*401(k)s and IRAs—Savings set aside usually for retirement. Often put into stocks and bonds to allow them to grow in value over the working years.

failed and even the U.S. government—the anchor of
international finance, which is blamed for causing the
disaster—has lost its credibility.

The purpose of this financial crisis is to take down the
United States and the U.S. dollar as the stable datum of
planetary finance and, in the midst of the resulting confu-
sion, put in its place a Global Monetary Authority—a
planetary financial control organization to "ensure this
never happens again."

Sound Orwellian? Sound conspiratorial? Sound too
evil or too vast to be real?

This entity is being moved forward by world leaders
"as we speak." It is coming and the pace is quickening.

A year ago, I saw an article in which the president of
the New York Federal Reserve Bank was calling for a
"Global Monetary Authority," or GMA, to deal with the
world's financial crisis. While I have been following international banking institutions for some time, this was
the clue that they were making their move.[22] I wrote an
article on it at the time.

By the way, as some may recall, the president of the
New York Fed last year was a man named Timothy
Geithner. Geithner was very involved in structuring the
booby-trapped TARP bailout with Paulson and Bernanke.[23]

Of course, now, he is the secretary of the Treasury of
the United States.

Change we can believe in.

Once Geithner started to push a global financial authority as the solution to the world's financial troubles, other world leaders and opinion-leading voices in international finance began to forward this message. It has been a PR campaign of growing intensity. Meanwhile, behind the scenes, the international bankers are keeping their hands on the throat of the credit markets, choking off lending while the planet's financial markets asphyxiate and become more and more desperate for a solution.

British prime minister Gordon Brown, who has taken the point on this, has said that the world needs a "new Bretton Woods."[24] This is the positioning for the GMA. (Bretton Woods, New Hampshire, was the location where world leaders met after the Second World War and established the international financial organizations called the International Monetary Fund [IMF] and the World Bank to help provide lending to countries in need after the war.[25])

Sir Evelyn de Rothschild called for improved (international) regulations,[26] while the managing director of the IMF suggested a "high level council of ministers capable of reaching agreements and implementing them."[27]

The former director of the IMF, Michael Camdessus, called on "the global village" to "urgently and radically" implement international regulations.[28]

As the crisis has intensified, so too have calls for a global financial policeman; and, of late, the PR has been directed in favor of—surprise—the Bank for International Settlements.

The person at the BIS who was primarily responsible for the creation of Basel II is Jaime Caruana. The BIS board has now appointed him as the general manager, the bank's chief executive position, where he will be in charge of dealing with the current financial crisis, which he had no small part in creating.[29]

A few well-chosen sound bites tell the story.

Following a recent IMF function, discussion centered on the fact that the BIS could provide effective market regulation, while the *Global Investor* magazine opined that "perhaps the Bank for International Settlements in Basel" could undertake the task of best dealing with the crisis in the financial markets.

The UK *Telegraph* is right out front with it:

Global financial crisis: does the world need a new banking 'policeman'?

… New global solutions are needed because the machinery of global economic governance barely exists…. It is time for a Bretton Woods for this century….

> ... The big question ... is whether it is time to establish a global economic "policeman" to ensure the crash of 2008 can never be repeated....

> ... The answer might already be staring us in the face, in the form of the Bank for International Settlements (BIS).... The BIS has been spot on throughout this.[30]

And so you see, this was a drill. This was a strategy: Bring in Easy Money Alan to loosen the credit screws; open the floodgates to mortgage loans to the seriously unqualified with the CRA; bundle these as securities; repeal Glass-Steagall and waive capital requirements for investment banks so the mortgage-backed securities could be sold far and wide; wait until the loans matured a bit and some became delinquent, and ensure the media spread this news as if Heidi Fleiss had had a sex-change operation; then slam in an international accounting rule that was guaranteed to choke off all credit and crash the leading economies of the world.

Ensure the right people were in the key places at the right time—Greenspan, Paulson, Geithner, and Caruana.

When the economic pain was bad enough, promote the theory that the existing financial structures did not work and that a Global Monetary Authority—a Bretton

Woods for the twenty-first century—was needed to solve the crisis and ensure this does not happen again.

Which is exactly where we are right now.

What Do You Do?

Let me preface this section by saying that this is advice designed to help you orient your assets—i.e., your reserves, your retirement plans, etc.—to the Brave New World of international finance. It is not meant as advice about what you do with your business, or your job, or your personal life.

Those things are all senior to this subject, which has a very narrow focus. There is an embarrassment of riches of materials that you can use to stay ahead of and on top of this crisis. Use them to flourish and prosper. This article is not a call to cut back or contract. It is to provide you information so you know what is going on and can plan.

Enough said.

First of all, while not likely, but just in case Timothy Geithner is shocked into some New Age epiphany and Ben Bernanke grows some real wisdom in his polished dome, this is what the government should do:

1. Cancel any aspects of Basel II that are causing banks to misevaluate their assets.

2. Remove the provision of TARP that permits the Fed to pay interest on deposits.

3. Mandate that any funds given under the TARP bailout or that are to be given to banks in the future must be used to lend to deserving borrowers.

4. Repeal the Community Reinvestment Act.

5. Reinstate Glass-Steagall.

6. Restore mandated capital requirements to investment banks.

7. And in case Congress decides to cease being a flock of frightened sheep and take responsibility for the country's monetary policy, they should get rid of the privately owned Federal Reserve Bank and establish a monetary system based on production and property.

8. But if a Global Monetary Authority is put in place, it should not be controlled by central bankers. It should be fully controlled directly by governments with real oversight over it and with a system of checks and balances. This you can communicate when this matter hits Congress or the White House or both (which it almost certainly will).

And what do you do with your reserves in this Brave New World of international finance?

Modesty aside, please do what I have been recommending for a few years now: get liquid (out of the stock and bond markets) and put some of your assets into precious metals, gold and silver, but more heavily into silver.

Keep the rest in cash (CDs and T-bills) and perhaps a small bit in some stronger foreign currencies like the Swiss franc or Chinese yuan (also referred to as the RMB, which is short for renminbi).

And remember that my recommendations are based on my thirty years of experience in banking, finance, and investments, but I have no crystal ball and make no guarantees regarding my recommendations.

We are living in the most challenging economic times this planet has ever seen. I hope this article has helped shed some light on what is currently happening on the international financial scene. I didn't cover everything or everyone involved, but these are the broad strokes.

If you want to follow these shenanigans, log on to The London Summit 2009 (http://www.londonsummit .gov.uk/en/). It will all look and sound very reasonable— all about saving jobs and homes—but you have seen behind the wizard's curtain, and the above is what is really going on.

Keep your powder dry.

2
Hitler's Bank Goes Global

May 2009

Publisher's Note: *This is the article that notes the date of the coup with the creation of the Financial Stability Board (FSB). The FSB is the global monetary authority Wolfe mentioned in chapter 1. On April 2, 2009, when the G-20* signed the communiqué from the BIS in Basel, the FSB was born. It marks the date that Big Banker effected the hostile takeover of global finances, including the takeover of the American economy.*

A towering citadel housing what is essentially a sovereign state known as the Bank for International Settlements is located in Basel, Switzerland. The bank now controls the financial affairs of planet Earth.

If you think this is an exaggeration or the conspiratorial ramblings of the author . . . or not, I invite you to read on.

The Purpose of the Financial Crisis

I wrote the first installment of this article—"The Financial Crisis: A Look Behind the Wizard's Curtain"—in mid-March of this year.

---

*G-20—A group of twenty (G-20) finance ministers and central bank governors, established in 1999.

The article included the following statement:

"The purpose of this financial crisis is to take down the United States and the U.S. dollar as the stable datum of planetary finance and, in the midst of the resulting confusion, put in its place a Global Monetary Authority—a planetary financial control organization 'to ensure this never happens again.'"

This purpose has now been accomplished.

The dollar, the former king of currencies, now goes begging in the pant-suited persona of Hillary Clinton to our creditors at the Chinese Communist Party.[1]

Almost unthinkable a few short years ago, the U.S. dollar is fast losing its status as the world reserve currency, and any thought of saving it is being nuked by the Bernanke, Geithner, and Summers commitment to their Alice-in-Wonderland trillion-dollar budget deficits.

I would not be surprised to see central banks start using the renminbi (the currency of the newly awakened People's Republic of China—also called the yuan) for international trade and reserves in the not too distant future. This prediction will likely be scoffed at by global economists, but then they have about as much credibility as Larry, Moe, and Curly these days.

A more generally discussed alternative is the International Monetary Fund's SDR (which stands for Special Drawing Rights). There is no production or property behind the SDR. It is one of those clown currencies that are made up out of thin air—a magic trick central bankers like to do. Intoxicated by the power of the purse, they think of themselves as fiscal alchemists.

But the dollar has seen its glory. It can return one day, if Washington ever finds its financial backbone. But let's be real, with the exception of a very few, like Ron Paul in the House and Tom Coburn in the Senate, these folks are addicted to spending like junkies on horse.

More importantly, the other shoe has dropped. Like some ghoulish predator from another *Alien* sequel, a Global Monetary Authority has been born. It lives.

The Financial Stability Board

On April 2, 2009, the members of the G-20 (a loose-knit organization of the central bankers and finance ministers of the twenty major industrialized nations) issued a communiqué that gave birth to what is no less than Big Brother in a three-piece suit.[2]

Which means? . . .

The communiqué announced the creation of the all-too-Soviet-sounding Financial Stability Board (FSB)—and no, I'm not going to make a crack about the fact that this acronym is the same as that of the Russian intelligence service that replaced the KGB.

The Financial Stability Board. Remember that name well, because they now have control of the planet's finances . . . and, when one peels the onion of the communiqué, control of much, much more.

The FSB morphed into existence from an earlier incarnation called the Financial Stability Forum. The Financial Stability Forum (FSF) was established in 1999 to promote international financial stability through co-operation in financial supervision and surveillance. Since it had done such a wonderful job, the central bankers decided to expand its powers and give it a new name.[3]

A *board* sounds like it has more authority than a *forum.* But the name change isn't the problem. The FSB's broadened mandate includes, under point five:

> As obligations of membership, member countries and territories commit to pursue the maintenance of financial stability, maintain the openness and transparency of the financial sector, implement international financial standards (including the twelve key International Standards and Codes), and agree to undergo periodic peer reviews, using among other evidence IMF/World Bank public Financial Sector Assessment Program reports.[4]

Rather a mouthful of elitist banker-speak. But, as a friend of mine is fond of saying, "The devil is in the details."

The Twelve International Standards and Codes

While several press releases from the G-20's London conclave reference these codes as though they were handed down from a fiscal Mount Sinai, finding the specifics takes some digging.

But then the Bank for International Settlements (BIS), out of which the FSB operates, has never seen transparency as one of its core values. In fact, given its fascist pedigree, transparency hasn't been a value at all. Known as Hitler's bank, the Bank for International Settlements worked arm in arm with the Nazis, facilitating the transfer of gold from Nazi-occupied countries to the Reichsbank, and kept its lines open to the international financial community during the Second World War.[5]

As noted in the first article, the BIS is completely above the law.

It is like a sovereign state. Its personnel have diplomatic immunity for their persons and papers. No taxes are levied on the bank or the personnel's salaries. The grounds are sovereign, as are the buildings and offices. The Swiss government has no legal jurisdiction over the bank and no government agency or authority has oversight over its operations.

In a 2003 article titled "Controlling the World's Monetary System: The Bank for International Settlements," Joan Veon wrote:

> The BIS is where all of the world's central banks meet to analyze the global economy and determine what course of action they will take next to put more money in their pockets, since they control the amount of money in circulation and how much interest they are going to charge governments and banks for borrowing from them. . . .
>
> When you understand that the BIS pulls the strings of the world's monetary system, you then understand that they have the ability to create a financial boom or bust in a country. If that country is not doing what the money lenders want, then all they have to do is sell its currency.[6]

And if you don't find that troubling, a close reading of the new powers of the FSB is chilling.

The twelve key International Standards and Codes, which are minimum requirements, contain such things as

- clear specification of the structure and functions of government;

- statistical and data gathering from ministries of education, health, finance, and other agencies;

- corporate governance principles;

- shareholder rights;

- personal savings;

- secure retirement incomes;

- international accounting standards to be observed in the preparation of financial statements;

- international standards of auditing;

- securities settlement;

- foreign exchange settlement;

- minimal capital adequacy for banks;

- risk management;

- ratification and implementation of UN instruments; and

- criminalizing the financing of terrorism.

"Sounds oppressive," you say. "But I don't really care what a bunch of bankers do in Basel, Switzerland. It's got nothing to do with me." However, I am writing this to tell you that it has everything to do with you, your family, your business, your country, and—if you're up to it—your planet.

Because as currently structured, the dictates of the Financial Stability Board will impact your life without any say-so on your part whatsoever. Here's one example from an article written by former Clinton advisor and political strategist Dick Morris in an article for *The Bulletin* on April 6, 2009.

> The FSB is also charged with "implementing . . . tough new principles on pay and compensation and to support sustainable compensation schemes and the corporate social responsibility of all firms."
>
> That means that the FSB will regulate how much executives are to be paid and will enforce its idea of corporate social responsibility at "all firms."[7]

You begin to see what's involved here.

You see, these standards and codes are commitments, obligations, and requirements, not merely advice. The strategy, policies, and regulations of the FSB are worked out at the senior levels of the bank. They are approved by the plenary (the members of a body collectively) and implemented through the national representatives.

The Structure

The plenary, in this sense, is the complete membership body of the FSB. And the membership, my friends—the national representatives who implement these policies—just happen to be the heads of the planet's most powerful central banks. And in case it slipped your mind, most central banks are private institutions and answerable to no one.

Take our central bank, the Federal Reserve Bank. Yes, the chairman is appointed by the president and often testifies before Congress, but there is virtually no public control over the institution. It can't be audited nor can Congress tell it what to do. It is not really accountable to anyone.[8] The idea that the Fed is a government agency subject to the control of Congress is a PR line. It is simply not true.

Among other things, central banks govern a country's monetary policy and create (print) the country's money. They make income by charging interest on the money they loan to the government.

Watch this, because if you blink, you'll miss it.

Governments are perpetually in debt. They are always borrowing money. They have a mental disorder that prevents them from spending less than they collect in taxes—BDD, Budget Deficit Disorder. And if it looks like they might balance the books some year, why, someone can always start a war.

Here's an example.

Let's say the annual budget calls for the U.S. government to spend $2.5 trillion. But the income will only be $2 trillion. They're going to be a little short. But no worries, they have the ultimate credit card—a debt limit that they themselves control. If they borrow up to the established limit, they can just vote it higher—which they have done to the tune of a cool $11.2 trillion dollars.

The Fed loves this.

Listen as the secretary of the Treasury calls the chairman of the Fed.

"Ben. It's Tim."

"Dude. What's happening?"

"I need a little bread. Friggin' Taliban again."

"No problem, Timbo. How much you looking for?"

"Five hundred big ones."

Ben licks his lips. "Anything for you, big guy. Send me the notes and I'm down with the five hundred. Five percent work for you?"

"Whatever."

So the Treasury prints up $500 billion dollars' worth of IOUs—they are called Treasury bills (short term), notes (medium term), or bonds (long term)—and sends them over to the Fed with a fifth of Chivas.

In the old days, the Fed would print the cash. These days, they click a mouse.

Now here's the part where you aren't allowed to blink.

When the Fed prints the money or clicks the mouse, they have no money themselves. They are just creating it out of thin air. They just print it, or send it digitally. And then they charge interest on the money they *lent* to the Treasury. A hundred-dollar bill costs $0.04 to print. But the interest is charged on the $100. Go ahead: read it again; the words won't change.

The interest on the national debt last year (2008) was $451,154,049,950.63.[9] That's $1.23 billion a day. These are the same people that are now running our banks, insurance companies, and automobile manufacturers.

But I digress.

Sure, I oversimplified it. The Fed doesn't own all the debt and they do some other things. But these are the basics. That is how a central bank works.

It is the heads of the planet's central banks and some finance ministers that make up the membership of the FSB.

In brief, here's how it works: the board's leadership provides strategies, policies, and regulations to the membership. The members vote on the matters and then see to their implementation in their respective countries.

FSB leadership is in the hands of the chairman, Mario Draghi. Mr. Draghi is also the governor of Italy's central bank. He is a former executive director of the World Bank and like his comrade in international finance Henry Paulson—the former U.S. secretary of the Treasury who bludgeoned Congress out of the first $700 billion bailout package—Draghi was a managing director of Goldman Sachs until 2006. Like Paulson, he left Goldman in 2006, a year before the financial crisis exploded: Paulson went to Washington to run the U.S. Treasury; Draghi went to Rome to run Italy's financial system as well as the Financial Stability Forum (forerunner to the Financial Stability Board).

Let's call it government by Goldman, shall we?

The Real Situation

More to the point, you may have noticed that you weren't consulted on this setup. Neither was Congress. In other words, the command channel for implementing global financial strategies goes from the FSB leadership to its central banker members and from them to the world's financial institutions. You don't get a peek, neither does Congress, nor, for that matter, does the White House.[10]

And while there may be some accountability in some of the member countries, by and large these central bankers have the authority to implement these regulations and strategies. And they are held responsible by the FSB to do so.

In short, on April 2, 2009, the president signed a communiqué that essentially turned over financial control of the country, and the planet, to a handful of central bankers, who, besides dictating policy covering everything from your retirement income to shareholder rights, will additionally have access to your health and education records.

There is also this troubling little line about *"clear specification of the structure and functions of government."*

There is no oversight here. Not by you, not by Congress, not by anybody. No oversight over a handful of central bankers who operate out of a clandestine organization that is above the law and is responsible for having implemented and enforced the "standards" that froze world credit markets and precipitated the worst financial crisis in the planet's history (see "The Financial Crisis: A Look Behind the Wizard's Curtain").

This is nothing short of a full-blown *coup d'état*— a takeover of the world's financial systems. There were no wild-eyed revolutionaries brandishing AK-47s or machetes stained with the blood of the status quo. The coup was accomplished with the feigned civility of Armani-clad politicians in polished mahogany conference rooms turning their countries' financial autonomy over to a cabal of bankers in Basel, Switzerland, with the stroke of a pen.

I haven't heard word one out of Congress about this, but I'm afraid they are a few clowns short of a circus up there.

Which begs the question, what the hell do we do about this?

The Solution

There are two critical things that need to be done.

The first lies in the fact that the communiqué signed by the president is an agreement that is binding on the United States and, as such, requires approval by Congress. If classed as a *treaty*, it requires approval by two-thirds of the Senate. At the very least, approval should be by *congressional-executive agreement*, which requires a majority of both houses of Congress.[11]

The agreement signed in London on April 2, 2009, has been called a New Bretton Woods (Bretton Woods being the location of a meeting of world leaders toward the end of the Second World War, which gave birth to the international financial organizations the World Bank and the International Monetary Fund). The original Bretton Woods agreement was put in place as a congressional-executive agreement.[12] So this "New Bretton Woods" should at least do the same.

This step is just to get Congress to recognize their responsibility here. The Federal Reserve Act, the bill that established the Federal Reserve System, was passed in 1913 two nights before Christmas by a sparsely attended Congress.

People have been complaining about this ever since.

What do you say we don't let this happen again? Not on our watch. Congress needs to understand that it has a responsibility to approve any agreement signed by the president that is binding on this nation.

But the point is not to just get Congress to approve what has been done. It is to get them to recognize first that agreements have been made that affect our entire financial system, and second that it is their responsibility to shape these agreements in a way that is beneficial to our Republic *and* to provide a mechanism for real oversight of this international body.

Central bankers should not be making decisions about international finance without oversight and a system of checks and balances that are reflective of those provided by a republican form of government.

I am, of course, not talking about a political party here. No, no. I'm talking about the American form of government where citizens elect others to represent them.

A republican form of government is one that is operated by representatives chosen by the people.

Congress must step up to the plate. They must insist that the Financial Stability Board be ratified either by treaty or congressional-executive agreement. And that ratification must include the creation of a body with oversight and corrective powers that is comprised of representatives of all the nations involved who are chosen from each country's elected officials.

There is nothing inherently evil about an international financial organization. As much as we might protest it, it is a global world today, and a body that oversees the smooth flow and interchange of currencies and other financial instruments is needed in today's world.

But the organization cannot be controlled by international bankers who are not answerable to the citizens of the countries in which they operate. It should be overseen by a senior-level group which itself is organized as a liberal republic, following the original model of the United States.

Why? Because the system of government originally created by the United States has been the most successful form of government in man's history. Any problems with the system have come about as a result of deviations from the original structure—a representative form of government with adequate checks and balances.

Such a body could help create an international economic system in which those that want to be successful can be so. It would also allow them to take an active role in controlling their futures by effectively participating in the legislative process.

ACT!

Let your representatives and senators know: the Financial Stability Board must be approved by Congress *and* must be subject to oversight by elected officials of the countries involved.

Personal visits, followed by calls and faxes to both Washington and local offices, are the most effective. Don't be surprised if they don't know what you're talking about. Politely insist they find out and take action. And understand this when dealing with legislators or their staffs: they are focused almost exclusively on legislation that has already been introduced—a bill with a number on it.

That is not the case here. You want them to take action on this matter by introducing legislation that brings the approval and structure of the Financial Stability Board under congressional control.

This can be accomplished.

> "All tyranny needs to gain a foothold is for people of good conscience to remain silent."
> —*Thomas Jefferson*

Find your elected officials here:
http://www.visi.com/juan/congress/
and let them know what they need to do. After all, they
work for you.

3
The Financial Crisis:
The Hidden Beginning

June 2009

Publisher's Note: *This article was written three months after the original article, "A Look Behind the Wizard's Curtain." As Wolfe continued to do his research on the global crisis, he realized that there was an earlier beginning to the story than what he had presented in the first article. What follows is an account of the events that led up to the first Basel Accord, Basel I.*

On April 2, 2009, control of the planet's banks was turned over to the secret decisions of eleven men—board members of a Swiss organization with a troubling Nazi past.

Banking wasn't always that way....

My secretary would come into my office every morning at 9:00 a.m. with a room-service smile and an armload of computer printouts.

She would place the reports on my desk as if she were serving a fine meal and arrange them just so, with the over-draft (OD) report on top, and then slip out of the office as if she were trying not to wake anyone.

The customer's name was on the left side of the page followed by the date the account was opened, the six-month average balance, and a listing of the offending checks that had sentenced the account to the OD report. The amount of the checks and the total overdraft were featured prominently on the right-hand side of the page like perps in a police lineup.

The decisions were twofold: do I pay the checks and, whether paid or not, do I assess overdraft charges? Overdraft charges have gotten rapacious in recent years, but they were $4.00 an item back then, and believe it or not, it takes time, money, and effort for bank personnel to track down the impostor and send it home branded with banking's scarlet letter—*insufficient funds.*

I would usually let the charges stand, but I was not a tough close if someone called in with a plausible story on why the check beat the deposit to their account. This was usually good for one round of reversed OD charges, but rarely repeated despite screenplay-quality presentations.

A friend of mine had a leather shop down the street where he handcrafted sandals, belts, and wallets adorned with peace symbols, which, in those days, were found on everything from condoms to dog collars. He was of the genus *Hippy*, drove a ratty VW van covered in flowery orange and yellows, and wore iconic bell-bottomed Levi's. There was great profit in leather goods, but Jimmy paid no attention to his bank balance and overdrew the account with such regularity I sometimes wondered if he was trying to ensure the branch remained profitable.

Banking was more personal then:

"Jimmy, you're OD again."

"That's bullshit, man."

"No, Jimmy. It's not bullshit. You're overdrawn $312."

"I can't be overdrawn. I just gave you guys a bunch of bread. You probably held it so some checks would come in first and you could hit me with a bunch of overdraft charges."

"Lay off the weed, Jimmy. When did you make the deposit?"

"Yesterday. Seven hundred bones. Gave it to that foxy black chick with the Afro."

"Yes. I see it. But you're still OD."

"You're bummin' me out, man, really bummin' me out."

"When was the last time you reconciled your account, Jimmy?"

"Don't put that on me, man. That form is a bad trip. Gives me a migraine."

"Bring your last three statements down to the branch, and I'll have bookkeeping reconcile the account for you."

"Groovy. You gonna reverse the OD charges?"

"Not a prayer. Bring $312 with you."

"Fascist."

Your local bank was also where you went to get a loan to buy your new home. And there it stayed until it was paid off.

A customer would come into the branch, fill out an application, and, if approved, we would finance 75–80 percent of the purchase. The borrower would come up with the balance. When the loan was approved, we would issue the funds to escrow at the appropriate time and put the loan on our books, where it would stay, earning the bank the going rate of interest for home loans.

I'm sure there are still some community banks that offer personal service instead of having you talk to someone in the Philippines about your credit card, but I wrote this to make the point that banking—and mortgage banking in particular—has changed.

Banks started selling loans to investors while keeping the servicing. In other words, the borrower would keep making his mortgage payments to the bank that made the loan but the payment would be sent on to the investor who had purchased the loan from the bank. The investors were usually pension plans or large investment funds.

But this change in mortgage lending was just beginning.

A group of leading bankers would soon turn mortgage banking into a cancer that would eat the industry alive. What follows is the earlier beginning to our story "The Financial Crisis: A Look Behind the Wizard's Curtain"— a chronicle of the men and institutions who designed the current crisis: a crisis by design.

The Japanese

It was 1985, and the Land of the Rising Sun had become the planet's largest creditor nation.* Words like *Toyota, Panasonic,* and *Yamaha* had become part of the lexicon in places such as Omaha, Cleveland, and Des Moines. In 1970, the ten largest banks in the world were American. By the end of the eighties, six of the ten largest banks in the world were Japanese.

What happened?

The Japanese banks were pampered and protected by their government like corporate rock stars. They were permitted to operate with small amounts of reserve capital, which gave them an advantage over other banks and enabled them to expand their market share at the expense of their competition—the major money-center banks in New York and London represented by the dual-headed Darth Vaders of international finance, the U.S. Federal Reserve Bank and the Bank of England.[1]

The Gunfight at the O.K. Corral had nothing on what was about to occur to the banking samurai of Tokyo.

In the eighties, governments had varying regulations about how much capital their banks had to maintain. These standards were supposed to ensure that banks had

---

*Creditor nation—When a country exports more than it imports, it has a balance of payments surplus. When it imports more than it exports it becomes a debtor nation.

enough in reserves to protect themselves and their depositors against bad loans.

These "capital adequacy standards" were set as a percentage of the bank's assets. In other words, if the capital requirements were 8 percent and a bank had $8,000,000 in capital, they could expand their balance sheet to $100,000,000 in assets (loans and other investments).

But let's say the capital requirements were 4 percent. Taking the same bank with the same $8,000,000 in capital, they could carry $200,000,000 in loans and other assets, generating a great deal more income and profit for the bank.

If the capital requirements were 10 percent, that same bank could have assets of $80,000,000—fewer loans, less income.

You get the picture: the capital requirements dictated what amount of assets the bank could carry. And the amount of assets determined how much income the bank could generate.

The Japanese banks had low capital requirements—one central banker reported them to be as low as 3 percent. Others claimed 6 percent.[2] But in either case, they were low. The low capital requirements enabled them to hold more assets, which in turn spun off more income. The elevated income enabled them to offer lower interest rates on loans than the competition could. Their market share grew.

In time, Japanese banking became the Godzilla of international finance—a condition that did not sit well with Alan Greenspan, the recently appointed chairman of the Federal Reserve Bank, who dealt with the matter like a Mafia chieftain whose turf had been violated by the *yakuza*.

As soon as he assumed the throne at the Fed, Greenspan, complaining about advantage enjoyed by the Japanese banks, went to his comrades in coin at the Bank of England and executed a two-party agreement establishing capital adequacy standards for U.S. and UK banks.[3] The two of them then turned on their pinstriped Nipponese brothers and told them that they were going to be excluded from Western markets unless they agreed to an international standard of capital adequacy.

The Japanese, dragged to the agreement like a dog to a bath, signed the agreement on July 15, 1988, along with the central bankers of nine other industrialized nations, setting forth "international . . . regulations governing the capital adequacy of international banks."[4]

The agreement was signed at the secretive Bank for International Settlements in Basel, Switzerland, and was referred to as the Basel Accord. However, since a second accord was signed in 2004 (which we deal with in "Behind the Wizard's Curtain"), this agreement is now referred to as Basel I and the 2004 agreement as Basel II.

The Bank for International Settlements

I have dealt with the Bank for International Settlements in the two previous articles on the financial crisis and am going to take the liberty of quoting from them here. First, "A Look Behind the Wizard's Curtain":

> Central banks . . . govern a country's monetary policy and create that country's money.
>
> The Bank for International Settlements (BIS), located in Basel, Switzerland, is the central bankers' bank. There are fifty-five central banks around the planet that are members, but the BIS is controlled by a board of directors, which is comprised of the elite central bankers of eleven different countries (U.S., UK, Belgium, Canada, France, Germany, Italy, Japan, Switzerland, the Netherlands, and Sweden).
>
> Created in 1930, the BIS is owned by its member central banks, which, again, are private entities. The buildings and surroundings that are used for the purpose of the bank are inviolable. No agent of the Swiss public authorities may enter the premises without the express consent of the bank. The bank exercises supervision and police power over its premises. The bank enjoys immunity from criminal and administrative jurisdiction.

In short, they are above the law.

And from the second article, "Hitler's Bank Goes Global":

But then the Bank for International Settlements (BIS) . . . has never seen transparency as one of its core values. In fact, given its fascist pedigree, transparency hasn't been a value at all. Known as Hitler's bank, the Bank for International Settlements worked arm in arm with the Nazis, facilitating the transfer of gold from Nazi-occupied countries to the Reichsbank, and kept its lines open to the international financial community during the Second World War. . . .

It is like a sovereign state. Its personnel have diplomatic immunity for their persons and papers. No taxes are levied on the bank or the personnel's salaries. The grounds are sovereign, as are the buildings and offices. The Swiss government has no legal jurisdiction over the bank and no government agency or authority has oversight over its operations.

Basel I

Basel I established the terms for the minimum capital requirements for the ten central banks that signed the accord: Belgium, Canada, France, Italy, Japan, the Netherlands, the UK, the U.S., Germany, and Sweden (Switzerland signed later).

A standard had been set: banks had to maintain capital of 8 percent of their assets. But according to the agreement, all assets were not the same. Basel I introduced a special system of weighing the risk of different kinds of assets and loans—they referred to it as risk-weighted assets. For example, corporate loans to businesses called for a higher percentage capital than mortgage loans.[5] As a consequence, banks started cutting back on corporate loans and seeking ways to expand their mortgage portfolios.[6]

As for the Japanese banks, they had to adjust. But the Nikkei Index (the Japanese stock market) was booming at the time, so they didn't consider it a big problem. Between 1984 and 1989, the Nikkei had risen from 11,500 to 38,900. As stocks increased in value, the capital base of the Japanese banks (made up largely of stock) increased as well.[7]

Things were cool. Sake flowed, geishas danced, and banker-*san* was happy. But the good times were short lived. Less than a year later, in May of 1989, the Nikkei began a decline that eventually brought the index down to below 8,000.[8]

As went the Nikkei, so went the capital structure of the banks. Down they went, slashing their ability to lend and sending the entire Japanese economy into a recession that has been called the "lost decade."

You don't cross the Fed and the Bank of England and get away with it. Not on this planet.

It was a different story for the U.S. banks. The new capital adequacy standards laid down as Basel I had loopholes through which the American bankers were able to drive their Porsches to bonuses larger than the budgets of several third-world countries.

The Intentions of Basel I

Writers have referred to the consequences of Basel I as unintended.

Were they really?

Greenspan not only sat on the board of directors of the Bank for International Settlements, he was also of course the chairman of the Federal Reserve Bank. From this position he kept interest rates suppressed at abnormally low levels, ushering in a lethal binge of credit excess in America; advanced the Community Reinvestment Act, which mandated mortgage lending to anyone who drew breath (and some who didn't); and, along with Robert Rubin and Larry Summers, actively fought efforts to regulate the exploding market in toxic financial instruments called derivatives.

This included using his influence to help eliminate laws that had been on the books for decades protecting people from speculative excess and abuse in financial markets (see "The Financial Crisis: A Look Behind the Wizard's Curtain").

Derivatives

Derivatives are what Warren Buffet has called "financial weapons of mass destruction"—financial products that seem to have been imported from a galaxy far, far away.[9]

Derivatives are financial instruments that *derive* their value from some underlying asset. An example of a derivative is one you have heard a lot of lately: mortgage-backed securities.

Here's how this works. Mortgage loans are packaged up and legally pooled into a financial document called a security. This simply means that there is a formal certificate that represents a group of loans. The investor buys the security. The security pays interest to the investor, which is based on the interest rates of the underlying mortgages.

You can see where the name comes from: the financial instrument, the mortgaged-backed security, is *backed* by the mortgages.

It is a derivative because the financial instrument, the security, *derives* its value from the underlying assets (the mortgage loans).

So what were the intentions of the central bankers when they crafted Basel I? One was to take out the Japanese banks. Mission accomplished.

The other was obvious: to curtail lending to corporations while focusing the attention and appetites of those same lenders on the increased income and bonuses available by investing in mortgage-backed securities.

Under Basel I, banks only had to have half as much capital to invest in mortgages as was required for corporate loans. Or put another way, they could invest twice as much in mortgages as they could in corporate loans with the same amount of capital. The more loans, the more income.

What else did the bankers of Basel think was going to happen other than an explosion in mortgage lending? Nothing of course.

And later, when the lenders bought credit insurance for the securities, the capital requirements were reduced even further, pouring gas on what had by then become a raging inferno of credit speculation.

Credit Default Swaps

It wasn't actually called credit insurance, though. It had another one of those off-planet names, *credit default swaps*, but in essence that's what it was. Here's how this piece of the puzzle fit.

The bank would buy a contract from an insurer that covered the credit risk of the derivative. In other words, the bank would pay a fee to the insurance company—just like an insurance premium—and if the security turned bad, if the loans failed to pay, the insurance company was obligated to cover the bank's loss.[10]

When banks bought credit default swaps for their derivatives from an AAA-rated insurance company, the derivative itself took on an AAA rating.[11]

When the derivative received an AAA rating, the bank's capital requirements—already reduced because the derivatives were made up of mortgages—were reduced even more, freeing up more capital, which enabled them to buy more derivatives, which . . .

There were just a couple of small problems. The credit default swaps—not technically being insurance—were entirely unregulated. This meant that the insurance companies that issued these—think American Insurance Group (AIG), which was the world's largest insurance company and rated AAA, but which is now owned by thee and me—did not have to carry reserves to cover the loss if the trillions of dollars of derivatives they insured went bad.[12]

The other was the fact that with the passage of the Community Reinvestment Act, the mortgage market was awash in subprime loans (borrowers with poor credit, low income, and no or low down payments). And it was these loans that were packaged into mortgage-backed securities by the trillions and sold to virtually every major bank on the planet, making the international financial structure pregnant with disaster.

It was at this point, having originally set the stage, that the world's central bankers returned to the Bank for International Settlements in Basel, Switzerland, and issued a second set of rules referred to as Basel II. Included in the Basel II Accord was an accounting rule called *mark to market*, which brought the planet's entire financial system to its knees. (Mark to market is discussed in "Behind the Wizard's Curtain.") Mark to market was like pulling the pin on an enormous hand grenade made up of trillions of dollars of toxic derivatives.

On April 2, 2009, at a meeting of world leaders in London, the final card was played: terrified about the potential consequences of a planetary meltdown, they agreed to a plan that established a global financial dictatorship at the Bank for International Settlements called the Financial Stability Board. And this, dear friends, was the goal from the beginning.

If we are going to be realists, we must acknowledge that Greenspan—along with a few fellow monetary jihadists like Paulson, Rubin, Summers, and Geithner—planted the bomb in Basel I, lit the fuse by ensuring any meaningful protection against it was removed, and then detonated it with Basel II. What followed the explosion was a global financial coup, which was executed in April.

It took a while for the fuse to burn and the bomb to detonate, but when viewed as a well-constructed plan, the intentions seem inescapable: this financial crisis was and is a *crisis by design.*

The story of how Basel II created the worldwide financial crisis and how the Financial Stability Board was created is covered in detail in my earlier articles on this subject: "The Financial Crisis: A Look Behind the Wizard's Curtain" and "Hitler's Bank Goes Global."

4

The Goldman Connection

August 2009

There will be a war. I'm certain of it.

No, not with Iran, though I'd like to introduce Mahmoud "I refuse to wear a necktie under any circumstances" Ahmadinejad to a woman I met several years ago. She and her twin sister had been experimental subjects of Nazi madman Dr. Josef Mengele. Mengele had tried to change the color of their eyes with dye. The woman was blind. Her sister died at Auschwitz.

Mahmoud, who thinks the Holocaust was a hoax, forgot to pay his brain bill.

And they are a few sandwiches short of a picnic in Pyongyang. Still, I don't think the Chinese will let Kim Jong-il and his newly appointed secret-police-chief son, Kim Jong-un, drag the West into a military confrontation on the Korean peninsula. It's a little too close to home and a Korean War II is not part of Beijing's master plan. At least not yet.

No, this is a war brewing between two iconic American institutions that couldn't be more different: the voice of America's rock culture, *Rolling Stone* magazine, and the country's premier Armani-clad investment bank, Goldman Sachs.

Rolling Stone recently published an article called "The Great American Bubble Machine," a masterful exposé by Matt Taibbi revealing Goldman's greed and corruption in the creation of several investment "bubbles" that have made the firm and its partners—the term *filthy rich* comes to mind—but which have been devastating to Americans and to the U.S. economy.[1]

I rarely use those two words together. I have no problem with people making money—barrels of the stuff. Boatloads. But this needs to be done with some sense of ethics, some sense of morals, some sense of responsibility toward one's fellow man.

I was informed that Goldman is preparing a response. One wonders if the Wall Street veneer will crack: if they'll come out with their pinstripes pressed and PR guns blazing, trying to marginalize Taibbi.

As those of you who have followed my recent articles on the financial crisis know, I have pointed out the all-too-coincidental participation of Goldman executives in the creation of the financial crisis. Machiavelli himself would be proud of what has been nothing less than a bloodless takeover of the planet's financial systems. The Guys from Goldman have played their part.

While I have previously drawn attention to a few of the key figures, Taibbi has peeled the onion on several of the investment bank's schemes and has also laid bare the army of Goldman alumni that have turned up at critical decision points in the universe of credit, investment, and finance.

His orientation was such that he omitted a few names that I will cover below. But the article is exhaustively researched and ties Goldman to everything from the Great Depression to speculation in oil futures before last year's election that sent gas prices to $5.00 a gallon here in the land of many freeways. My focus, on the other hand, has been exposing the actual cause of the worldwide financial crisis. And our paths have crossed at a few key junctures.

Junctures that bring to mind the great Gordon Gekko—Michael Douglas's character in Oliver Stone's *Wall Street*. Preening in front of the board of directors and up and down the aisle among the shareholders of Teldar Paper, Douglas shares the philosophy of the successful investment banker as if handing down commandments from Mount Wall Street: "Greed is good. Greed is right. Greed works. Greed clarifies and cuts through and captures the essence of the evolutionary spirit."[2]

Yeah, baby.

But is it more than greed? Are Goldman Sachs alumni part of a broader agenda that has not only lined their pockets with the spoils of corruption that Taibbi has exposed but also helped facilitate an international financial coup—a coup that has put the control of the planet's financial affairs into the hands of a small group of central bankers that hold secret meetings at what is nothing less than the Vatican of international finance: the Bank for International Settlements located in Basel, Switzerland?

If you've had a suspicion that bankers are running Washington, then hang on to your Calvins because, while it starts in DC, this story is global in reach and is rolling out before your eyes—if you are willing to look.

Robert Rubin

I could start this part of the story with Henry Fowler, who, after serving as the thirty-fifth secretary of the Treasury, in 1969 became a partner at Goldman after leaving office. But that's not how things worked in the nineties and beyond. Oh no. The current sequence is very different.

Pictures of Robert Rubin always remind me of the cartoon character Droopy. He seems to be in a perpetual state of sad worry. Hard to know what he's worried about, having received fifty million in compensation from his last employer (Citigroup). Perhaps it's because the financial website *MarketWatch* recently named him as one of the "10 most *unethical* people in business."[3]

More to the point of our story, having served twenty-six years with Goldman Sachs, ascending to the position of co-chairman, Rubin came to Washington with the

Clinton administration as the assistant to the president for economic policy. Bill must have dug the Wall Street touch, because in January of 1995, he appointed Rubin the seventieth United States secretary of the Treasury.

This could be called the start of what the *New York Times* has referred to as the modern era of "Government Sachs."[4]

The hallmark of Rubin's years in Washington was deregulation—specifically, deregulation of the financial industry. Turn the financial industry loose. Let the big dogs eat. Let them earn. They have Porsche payments to make. Working with Greenspan, he kept interest rates implausibly low and ensured that regulatory safeguards were gunned down like victims in an L.A. drive-by shooting. The Glass-Steagall Act is a prime example. A piece of Depression-era legislation that kept investment banks and commercial banks from committing fiscal incest, it was repealed—charged with being out of touch with the global financial structure.

What it was out of touch with was an agenda to open the floodgates to unbridled speculation by banks that set the industry up for a financial Hiroshima.

It takes a great deal of power and influence to get a federal law repealed in this country—especially one that has served the country well for seventy years. But Rubin, with a little help from his friends—Larry Summers and Alan Greenspan—got it done.

These and other similar actions helped pave the way for an economic crisis that would soon engulf the entire planet.

> The housing bubble has burst. The financial services industry is a ward of the state. Insurance companies and automakers are tottering on the brink of bankruptcy. Consumer credit is drying up along with consumer confidence. Banks have stopped lending money, and big corporations have started laying workers off. The stock market is at a five-year low. But amid the greatest financial panic since the Great Depression, the market for one asset stubbornly resists correction: the immaculate reputation of Robert Rubin, former Treasury secretary and pre-eminent economic wise man of the Democratic Party.
>
> . . . But the financial deregulation that allowed markets to boil over began well before President George W. Bush took office. Three decisions relevant to the market meltdown . . . can be attributed to Rubin."
>
> —Timothy Noah[5]

Mexico

Let's set aside for the moment that when Rubin was co-chairman of Goldman, the firm underwrote billions of dollars in bonds for the Mexican government. When the Mexican peso tanked a few years later, Rubin, as secretary of the Treasury, arranged a multibillion-dollar taxpayer bailout, which, according to reports, saved Goldman a cool $4 billion. Kind of a dress rehearsal for Hank Paulson's trillion-dollar raid on the U.S. Treasury, which channeled tens of billions into the womb from which he came— Mother Goldman. But we'll get to that.

Rubin did more than pave the road to a financial Armageddon with Maestro Greenspan. His spawn have helped ensure that the crisis came off as planned and that it was *solved* with the creation of a global financial dictator, who—prepare to be shocked—is also a Goldman alum. But, again, I'm getting ahead of myself.

The Acolytes

Summers

At Treasury, Rubin groomed two protégés that helped craft the multitrillion-dollar financial bailout and that are today in charge of U.S. financial policy: Larry Summers and Timothy Geithner.

Summers, though not a formal Goldman alum, is a fully certified Rubin deregulation clone. He was *chief economist for the World Bank* in the early '90s and later served as Rubin's deputy secretary of the Treasury. When Rubin left, Summers took full control of Treasury for the last year and a half of the Clinton administration. Today Summers is the director of the National Economic Council, which means he is in the commanding position of being the senior advisor to President Obama on domestic and international economic policy.

Geithner

Timothy Geithner, like Summers, worked for Rubin at Treasury during the Clinton administration and was a Rubin favorite. He stayed on during Summers's tenure and then snagged the powerful presidency of the New York Federal Reserve Bank. It was Rubin who got Geithner the gig at the New York Fed and it was Rubin who hooked him up with Obama, who appointed him as his secretary of the Treasury.

In case there is any doubt about Geithner's loyalties, it is widely known on Wall Street and inside the Beltway that Goldman filed adoption papers on him years ago.

> In an interview on July 3, 2009, the former U.S. assistant secretary of the Treasury, Dr. Paul Craig Roberts, was asked, "Does the U.S. Treasury secretary work for the people or does he work for the banking system on Wall Street?" to which he replied, "He works for Goldman Sachs."[6]

So, for those who thought that Rubin had left the stage

of U.S. economic policy, think again. Because not only has Rubin himself been named as an advisor to President Obama, but another of his groupies, Christina Romer, has been named as the chair of the White House Council of Economic Advisors.

Even today, then, Goldman's former co-chairman is advising Obama behind the scenes and his acolytes are in charge of the U.S. Treasury (Geithner) and the White House Council of Economic Advisors (Romer) and the National Economic Council (Summers). The White House Council of Economic Advisors is made up of academicians who provide the president with economic statistics and other information on domestic and international financial matters. The National Economic Council brings together key administration players and agency heads to coordinate and see to the implementation of the administration's economic policy. The director (Summers) is the president's senior economic advisor.

You'd think with this crew in place, Goldman would have had the White House covered. But Obama apparently went for their two-for-one sale. In addition to Rubin, another *former Goldman chairman,* the controversial Jon Corzine, has been a top Obama economic advisor. In fact he was on the short list to become secretary of the Treasury. But Rubin ruled and Geithner got the gig.

Given that Goldman employees gave more money to Obama ($994,000) than any other commercial enterprise in the United States, and that the White House is awash in Goldmanites, it is no surprise that 1600 Pennsylvania Avenue is viewed as one of the bank's more important operating divisions.[7]

Patterson

Even with the White House under control, Geithner beefed up his G-man staff at Treasury. He named yet another Goldmanite as his chief of staff. Mark Patterson was selected to help him run the government's financial circus. Patterson gave up his plum position as the *vice president for Government Relations at Goldman*—meaning he was the investment bank's chief lobbyist—to become the number two man at Treasury.

I know, I know. Obama said no lobbyists in his administration; but, well, Mark is family. Sort of a fiscal fraternity brother—Alpha Delta Goldman.

Henry Paulson

But before Obama was Bush. And with oh-so-propitious timing, before the news of the financial crisis began to go mainline in 2007, a new *Goldman CEO* descended from his throne on Wall Street to come to Washington and help his government manage the nation's financial affairs.

We love you, Hank.

Viewed from the board rooms of Wall Street, Henry Paulson's blitzkrieg of the nation's capital was nothing short of stunning: a George Patton in pinstripes—except Patton was fighting a real enemy, not one that he himself had created.

Liar, Liar, Pants on Fire

At first, he used PR spin to calm the multitudes. As the crisis began to unravel in August 2007, Paulson assured the American people that the subprime mortgage problems were nothing to be concerned about, that they would remain contained due to the strong global economy.

> Reuters: U.S. Treasury Secretary Henry Paulson said on Wednesday that the market impact of the U.S. subprime mortgage fallout is largely contained and that the global economy is as strong as it has been in decades.[8]

Not.

The stock market peaked two months later followed by a crash that wiped out trillions.

In July of 2008, after the fall of IndyMac Bank, Paulson told the public that the banking system was safe and sound and that the situation was very "manageable."[9] Twenty-five banks failed in 2008. Sixty-four have gone under in the first six and a half months of 2009. Another 309 are now listed as "problem banks."[10]

In fact, according to FDIC chairman Sheila Bair, in March 2009, unless the FDIC gets more revenue, they themselves are going to be broke.

> "Without additional revenue beyond the regular assessments, current projections indicate that the fund balance will approach zero."[11]

In a television interview on *Meet the Press* on August 10, 2008, Paulson stated that he would not be putting any capital into Fannie Mae or Freddie Mac.* Three weeks later, he took them over and committed $200 billion in bailout funds; $60 billion has already been spent.[12]

When I was growing up, we'd call this kind of guy a "bullshit artist." But that didn't stop him from staging a raid on the U.S. Treasury in broad daylight that would have made Dillinger drool with envy. This, while Congress—a Democratic Congress at that—stood around with their thumbs up their butts.

---

*Fannie Mae, Freddie Mac—Federal National Mortgage Association, Federal Home Loan Mortgage Corporation. Fannie was established in 1938 to turn mortgages into securities to be sold to investors. Fannie dealt in the primary home loan market. Freddie was established in 1970 to compete with Fannie Mae to facilitate the secondary mortgage market. They were government-sponsored enterprises (GSEs); now they are in receivership held by the U.S. government.

Ed Liddy: AIG

Perhaps nothing quite so demonstrated this scam as the government bailout of American International Group (AIG), the country's largest insurance company. On September 16, 2008, Paulson coughed up $85 billion of your tax dollars to take control of AIG. The $85 billion loan got the government 80 percent ownership of the insurance giant. Just what I always wanted from my government, a bankrupt insurance company.[13]

It turns out the $85 billion wasn't enough. AIG has continued to hemorrhage losses and Uncle has now poured a total of $182 billion into the insurance company.

Jefferson and Adams weep.

Sticky constitutional issues aside, many have found it more than curious that when the government granted the loan, AIG turned right around and paid it out to the investment banks to which it owed money. The bank that got the largest payout was . . . of course, Goldman Sachs—a cool $13 billion.[14] The money simply passed from your paycheck to the U.S. Treasury, from the Treasury to AIG and from AIG to Goldman (and other banks).

Naturally, Paulson didn't provide the loan without ensuring that Goldman and fellow banksters would be repaid in full. No, no. He made sure the transfers would occur without any objection from AIG or unseemly negotiations with the banks.[15] To do this, he tapped *Goldman Sachs board member, Ed Liddy,* to be the new CEO of AIG.

The good-hearted Mr. Liddy took the gig for a dollar a year in salary from AIG. But he held on to his $3 million in Goldman stock.

Cute, eh?

Goldman made billions from AIG earlier as well. AIG didn't know this. Neither did Goldman's clients. You see, despite the fact that they had collected enormous fees selling financial products that were "insured" by AIG, Goldman simultaneously sold AIG short. You get this? On the one hand, they sold financial instruments to their clients, which carried high investment ratings because AIG insured the buyer against loss. At the same time, they made investment "bets" for their own account against AIG. Estimates are that they made $4.7 billion betting *against* AIG while *selling* the AIG-guaranteed products to their clients.

> "Greed clarifies and cuts through and captures the essence of the evolutionary spirit."
>
> — Gordon Gekko

AIG behind him, Hammering Hank marched on.

Lehman Brothers

Paulson had worked out strategies to have Bear Stearns purchased by J.P. Morgan in March of '08 and had committed $200 billion to rescue Freddie and Fannie in early September, but when Goldman's chief rival, Lehman Brothers, began to waver in midsummer, he turned a blind eye. Lehman went bankrupt and sent the already declining stock market into a colossal rout. The next day, he helped arrange an $85 billion bailout for AIG.

Following Lehman's collapse, Goldman and Morgan Stanley were the only remaining pure investment banks left on Wall Street.

The Bailout

Congress was next.

Attila the Hun had nothing on Paulson and his lap dog Ben Bernanke and their assault on Congress, with threats of riots and martial law as they fear-mongered the Troubled Asset Relief Program (TARP) through the House and Senate—winding up with a cool trillion dollars to "save" the banks.[16]

Congress's actions remind me of a bad Godzilla movie, with masses of panicked Japanese citizens fleeing the fire-breathing monster, which is lumbering through the city toppling buildings and devouring cars.

88   Crisis by Design

The legislation drafted by our elected officials sounds like something issued to Stalin by the Politburo. They granted Paulson complete dictatorial powers over the bailout money. The TARP read in part:

> Decisions by the Secretary pursuant to the author-
> ity of this Act are non-reviewable and committed to
> agency discretion, and may not be reviewed by any
> court of law or any administrative agency.[17]

Calling the multibillion-dollar bailout a "stimulus" pro-gram is but a cruel joke. This was nothing more compli-cated than another burglary in plain daylight—a theft of hundreds of billions of dollars from American taxpayers into the Armani-clad arms of major Wall Street banks.

You won't be surprised to learn, I'm sure, that Goldman Sachs got a cool $10 billion of TARP funds. And if you followed the billions pouring from your paychecks to Wall Street, you might remember that Bank of America at first received $25 billion. Then, in the midst of the chaos, they agreed to purchase Merrill Lynch. As it turned out, however, Merrill's losses were $15 billion more than B of A had expected. This was due in part to $4 billion in bonuses paid out by Merrill's CEO, John Thain, who pushed the bonuses through his books just before the Bank of America deal closed.[18]

Bank of America was taken by surprise by the losses and the purchase of Merrill Lynch started to go shaky, to which Comrade Paulson coughed up another $20 billion of your tax dollars.[19]

You guys are so cool bailing out these banks. I mean it. It brings tears to my eyes.

Oh, I should mention that John Thain, the guy who pushed through the last-minute billions in bonuses, had been the *president and co-chief operating officer at Goldman Sachs* before becoming the president of Merrill Lynch.

Robert K. Steel: Treasury to Wachovia

Another Goldman alum to drive his bank headlong into the merger-mania chaos of the financial crisis was Robert Steel. Steel had worked with Paulson at Goldman for thirty years and eventually rose to the position of *vice chairman* of the firm.

He followed Paulson to the U.S. Treasury in 2006 and became his top financial policy advisor. In July of 2008, he left the government and became the CEO of Wachovia bank, the sixth largest bank in the country.

How did he wind up at Wachovia? Three weeks earlier, Wachovia—who had paid Goldman Sachs $77 million in fees for financial advice—also sought their assistance in finding a new CEO.[20]

Steel was the man. Three short months later, Steel struck a deal with Citibank to buy Wachovia—a deal that required hundreds of billions in loan guarantees from the government. Then he changed his mind and sold Wachovia to Wells Fargo without the government involved and became a member of the Wells Fargo board of directors.

According to Taibbi's article:

> . . . Robert Steel, the former Goldmanite head of Wachovia, scored himself and his fellow executives $225 million in golden-parachute payments as his bank was self-destructing.[21]

Other articles claim that Steel himself did not take a bonus.

Regardless, you have Goldman getting millions in fees to advise Wachovia on, among other things, the selection of a new CEO, who, it turns out, is a former *Goldman vice chairman*. Nothing illegal about it, but the financial incest begins to smell pornographic.

Neel Kashkari: TARP Front Man

Paulson is nothing if not thorough. While he ultimately called the shots, he brought in someone else to oversee the allocation of the TARP funds and take the congressional heat. This was thirty-five-year-old *Goldman vice president*

Neel Kashkari, who, as the head of the Office of Financial Stability at Treasury, was in control of the $700 billion in bailout funds. It was Kashkari who had to testify about the TARP to Congress—a hot seat whose temperature started to soar shortly after Paulson's scam began to dawn on the legislators.

The Takeover

There were others. In fact, Paulson brought so many former Goldman executives to Treasury the *New York Times* noted the "appearance that the Treasury Department has become a de facto Goldman division."

These included

Reuben Jeffrey, a *former managing partner of Goldman's European Financial Institutions Group* in London;

Dan Jester, a *former Goldman vice president;*

Steve Shafran, *long-time Paulson associate at Goldman;*

Kendrick Wilson III, a *managing partner at Goldman in the Financial Institutions Group;* and

Edward Forst, a *former executive vice president and chief administrative officer at Goldman.*

Current or veteran Goldman executives all, they worked on everything from the bailout of Fannie and Freddie to the capital restructuring of the nation's banks.

All of which makes Andy Borowitz's satirical article in the July 16, 2009, *Huffington Post* that much more understandable. The lead reads:

> In what some on Wall Street are calling the biggest blockbuster deal in the history of the financial sector, Goldman Sachs confirmed today that it was in talks to acquire the U.S. Department of the Treasury.[22]

No surprise that the first two people I showed the article to thought it was real.

Joshua Bolten: The White House

Paulson and his Goldman gladiators also had air cover from the White House. George Bush's chief of staff during the bailout blizzard was none other than Josh Bolten. Bolten had become chief of staff in April of 2006 and is credited with persuading the president to recruit Paulson as the Treasury secretary.

No surprise, since Bolten had been the *executive director, Legal & Government Affairs for Goldman Sachs International* before joining the Bush 2000 presidential campaign.

Powerful friends. Powerful places.

But the Goldman virus has not been confined to the White House and the Treasury, not by a long shot.

The Derivatives Boom

Neil Levin

The acknowledged bogeymen of the world's financial crisis were mortgages, many of which were subprime, packaged up into investment products called mortgage-backed securities—also called derivatives because the package, the security, *derived* its value from the underlying mortgages. There is much more to this story (see "The Financial Crisis: A Look Behind the Wizard's Curtain"), but the point here is that these mortgages were a critical component to the crisis.

For reasons we detailed in a follow-up article, "The Financial Crisis: The Hidden Beginning," the explosive growth of these products was due in large part to the fact that the securities carried an AAA investment-grade rating. That rating was granted because Goldman Sachs and other banks were able to purchase what was essentially credit insurance for the investment. In other words, if the investment went bad, it was "insured" against loss.

This kind of protection was called a *credit default swap*. Though "swaps" looked like insurance and acted like insurance, they were remarkably adjudicated not to be so, thus eliminating the need for the "insurer" to hold reserves against possible losses. This opened the door to a torrent of speculation in the derivatives.

Let Matt Taibbi tell it.

> AIG, a major purveyor of default swaps, approached the New York State Insurance Department in 2000 and asked whether default swaps would be regulated as insurance. At the time, the office was run by one Neil Levin, a *former Goldman vice president*, who decided against regulating the swaps. Now freed to underwrite as many housing-based securities and buy as much credit-default protection as it wanted, Goldman went berserk with lending lust. By the peak of the housing boom in 2006, Goldman was underwriting $76.5 billion worth of mortgage-backed securities—a third of which were subprime—much of it to institutional investors like pensions and insurance companies.[23] [emphasis mine]

The Commodities Exchange

Gary Gensler

But not to worry. We're protected now. The regulation of many derivatives and other exotic financial instruments—the $5 trillion commodity futures industry (gold, silver, oil, treasury bills, corn, cotton, sugar, etc.)—has recently been delegated by President Obama to Gary Gensler.

Gensler was confirmed as the head of the Commodity Futures Trading Commission (CFTC) in May, but it took a little arm twisting. Some members of Congress had misgivings.

You see, back in 2000 when he was at Treasury, Gensler advocated legislation—which eventually passed— exempting credit default swaps and some other derivatives from regulation.

Still, it's hard to argue with his understanding of derivatives. He spent eighteen years at Goldman Sachs, the most aggressive derivative trader on Wall Street, where he became a *partner*. He subsequently went to the Treasury Department where he pushed for the deregulation of the industry. Now President Obama has put him in charge of it.

Change we can believe in . . .

The New York Stock Exchange

Duncan Niederauer

Goldman alumni control not only the commodities markets but the major stock markets of the world as well. In May of 2007, the granddaddy of stock markets, the New York Stock Exchange (NYSE), bought Euronext (a pan-European stock exchange with subsidiaries in Belgium, France, Netherlands, Portugal, and the United Kingdom), which, now branded as NYSE Euronext, operates the largest securities exchange on the planet.

To run the show, the newly combined entity brought in Duncan Niederauer and appointed him chief executive officer. Niederauer had been a *partner and managing director at Goldman Sachs* before joining NYSE Euronext.

The New York Fed

Stephen Friedman

The Federal Reserve System controls the country's money supply. Nice gig if you can get it. It is made up of a board of governors (seven), appointed by the president for fourteen-year terms. There are twelve Federal Reserve Banks around the country. The New York Fed is a first among equals. An institution of awesome power, it supervises and controls the major money center banks in New York, the capital of the U.S. financial industry.

The New York Fed worked closely with Treasury Secretary Paulson on numerous aspects of the bailout during the chaos of the financial meltdown in the fall and winter of '08.

Much of this work was carried out by Timothy Geithner, then president of the New York Fed, until Rubin helped get him the job as the secretary of the Treasury. The chairman of the New York Fed at this time was Stephen Friedman. He picked up the reins when Geithner left while looking for a replacement.

Friedman was a former *CEO of Goldman Sachs* and later *chairman* at Goldman. He'd left Goldman in 2002 to oversee economic policy in the Bush White House as the chairman of the National Economic Council. Later, Bush appointed him to the chairmanship of the President's Foreign Intelligence Advisory Board.

In 2004, he returned to New York and the chairmanship of the Fed. In addition, he returned to Goldman to become its chairman while he was also the chairman of the Federal Reserve Bank of New York.

William Dudley

To replace Geithner as president of the NY Fed, Friedman selected William Dudley. Dudley had been a *partner and managing director at Goldman Sachs* for ten years prior to the Fed appointment.

Incest doesn't begin to say it.

From the White House to Treasury, from the New York Fed to AIG, from the Commodity Futures Trading Commission to the New York Stock Exchange, Goldman is there.

The World Bank and the International Monetary Fund

Robert Zoellick

But it doesn't stop at our shores. It's a global economy today, which requires global control.

The World Bank was founded in 1945 to help with the reconstruction of Europe after the Second World War. Over the years, their mission changed.

Today they claim that their purpose is to eliminate world poverty—kind of a pinstriped Mother Theresa for the planet.[24] Unfortunately, this is at odds with what they actually do. If they were achieving their aims, the countries that they worked with would be prospering. But the reverse is true. In fact, an objective view of the results of the bank's activities leads one to the inescapable conclusion that what the World Bank produces is indebted nations.[25]

In their beneficence, the World Bank makes loans to third-world countries, countries that can't borrow elsewhere. The loans carry conditions that dictate domestic policy "adjustments" in health, education, tax policy, judicial matters, agriculture, manufacturing . . .

You get the picture. The bank and its sister organization, the International Monetary Fund, have about three-quarters of the planet in debt like this. Sarah

Anderson, the director of the Global Economy Program of the Institute for Policy Studies in Washington, DC, put an interesting spin on it:

> Medieval doctors always prescribed the same "cure"; no matter what the ailment, they applied leeches to patients and bled them. For the past decade and a half, critics have likened the World Bank and the International Monetary Fund (IMF) to these doctors. The two institutions have thrown millions of people deeper into poverty by promoting the same harsh economic reforms . . . regardless of local culture, resources, or economic context. Strapped with heavy debts, most developing countries have reluctantly accepted these reforms, known as structural adjustment programs (SAPS), as a condition for receiving IMF or World Bank loans.
>
> In recent years, the doctors' harsh medicine has been exposed in dozens of studies and in increasingly vocal street protests. In response, the World Bank and the IMF have been attempting to revamp their public image into that of antipoverty crusaders.[26]

The president of the World Bank is Robert Zoellick. In this position, Zoellick walks in the shoes of great humanitarians like über-neocon Paul Wolfowitz, "architect of the Iraq War," and Robert McNamara, the Johnny Appleseed of Agent Orange.[27]

Zoellick is in charge of spreading loans around the world to eliminate poverty, not unlike McNamara's blanketing of Southeast Asia with Agent Orange to stop Communism. Both agendas produce the same results—toxicity and, in some cases, death—of the corporal body or the body politic.

Prior to joining the World Bank, Zoellick served as *vice chairman, international, of the Goldman Sachs Group.*

You gotta love these guys.

The World Bank and the International Monetary Fund (whose current most powerful board member is our very own Timothy Geithner) are the key tacticians in ensuring that the planet's smaller economies remain deeply in debt. But they are no longer at the apex of international finance today.

As I have made clear in our earlier articles, the purpose of this financial crisis was to take down the United States and the U.S. dollar as the stable datum of planetary finance and, in the midst of the resulting confusion, put in its place a Global Monetary Authority—a planetary financial control organization to "ensure this never happens again."

This purpose has now been accomplished.

To explain how, I quote from an article I wrote on this subject a few months ago ("Hitler's Bank Goes Global").

The Financial Stability Board

On April 2, 2009, the members of the G-20 (a loose-knit organization of the central bankers and finance ministers of the twenty major industrialized nations) issued a communiqué that gave birth to what is no less than Big Brother in a three-piece suit.

The communiqué announced the creation of the all-too-Soviet-sounding Financial Stability Board (FSB). *The Financial Stability Board.* Remember that name well, because they now have control of the planet's finances . . . and, when one peels the onion of the communiqué, control of much, much more.

The Twelve International Standards and Codes

While several press releases from the G-20's London conclave reference these codes as though they were handed down from a fiscal Mount Sinai, finding the specifics takes some digging.

But then the Bank for International Settlements (BIS)—out of which the FSB operates—has never seen transparency as one of its core values. In fact, given its fascist pedigree, transparency hasn't been a value at all.

Known as Hitler's bank, the Bank for International Settlements worked arm in arm with the Nazis, facilitating the
transfer of gold from Nazi-occupied countries to the
Reichsbank, and kept its lines open to the international
financial community during the Second World War.

The BIS is completely above the law.

It is like a sovereign state. Its personnel have diplomatic
immunity for their persons and papers. No taxes are levied
on the bank or the personnel's salaries. The grounds are
sovereign, as are the buildings and offices. The Swiss
government has no legal jurisdiction over the bank and no
government agency or authority has oversight over its
operations.

In a 2003 article titled "Controlling the World's
Monetary System: The Bank for International Settlements,"
Joan Veon wrote:

> The BIS is where all of the world's central banks
> meet to analyze the global economy and determine
> what course of action they will take next to put
> more money in their pockets, since they control
> the amount of money in circulation and how
> much interest they are going to charge govern-
> ments and banks for borrowing from them. . . .
>
> When you understand that the BIS pulls the
> strings of the world's monetary system, you then

understand that they have the ability to create a financial boom or bust in a country. If that country is not doing what the money lenders want, then all they have to do is sell its currency.

And if you don't find that troubling, the Key International Standards and Codes just adopted by the Financial Stability Board cover such things as

- specification of the structure and functions of government;(!)
- data gathering from ministries of education, health, finance, and other agencies;
- matters dealing with personal savings accounts and retirement incomes.

Here's an example of the FSB in action, from an article written by former Clinton advisor and political strategist Dick Morris for *The Bulletin* on April 6, 2009.

> The FSB is also charged with "implementing . . . tough new principles on pay and compensation and to support sustainable compensation schemes and the corporate social responsibility of all firms."

> That means that the FSB will regulate how much executives are to be paid and will enforce its idea of corporate social responsibility at "all firms."

Almost no one on the planet has grasped what has occurred here.

Most central banks are answerable to no one. The U.S. Federal Reserve, for instance, is a private bank. It is owned by shareholders. Yes, the president appoints the chairman, and the chairman must testify before Congress, but no one gives them orders or tells them what to do. Again, they are a private, not government, institution (a very good reason to support Ron Paul's bill [H.R. 1207] calling for congressional authority to audit the Fed—something they currently have no right to do).

And it is the newly created Financial Stability Board, operating as an arm of the Bank for International Settlements, that *now structures and dictates the rules and regulations to be carried out by the central banks* of the world.

And given the fact that central banks essentially operate independently of their national congresses or parliaments, the FSB *now controls the monetary policy of the planet.*

It is now, for all practical purposes, the Politburo of international finance. And who is the chairman of this little known entity based in Basel, Switzerland? Mario Draghi. Draghi was a *partner at Goldman Sachs* until, like Henry Paulson, he left Goldman in 2006. Paulson took over the U.S. Treasury and Draghi became the governor of the Bank of Italy (Italy's central bank) and, in April of this year, chairman of the Financial Stability Board.

Goldman Alumni in Control

Draghi is also a member of the board of directors of the Bank for International Settlements. In fact, the BIS board reads like a Goldman reunion committee:

Mark Carney had a thirteen-year career with Goldman Sachs, where he became the *managing director of Investment Banking* before becoming the governor of the Bank of Canada and a member of the BIS board.

William Dudley, president of the New York Fed and *former partner at Goldman Sachs,* is also a member of the board, along with Draghi.

And there you have it. *Goldman alumni* in complete financial control of U.S. financial policy and markets, from the White House and Treasury to the New York Fed, the New York Stock Exchange, and the Commodity Futures Trading Commission. At the international level, they are in positions of power at the World Bank, the International Monetary Fund, the Bank for International Settlements, and its newly created fiscal overlord, the Financial Stability Board.

This is my fourth article in a series about the financial crisis. Despite our exposure of what some commentators have called Goldman's economic terrorism, it is important to understand that they are but a part—soldiers in pin-stripes—of a more basic agenda, which is nearly complete at this point.

This agenda is set forth in my previous articles—
"A Look Behind the Wizard's Curtain," "Hitler's Bank
Goes Global," and "The Hidden Beginning."

But "nearly complete" is not a *fait accompli*. And so I
refer you again to articles one and two, the closing para-
graphs of both set out specific actions to take to help bring
this situation under control.

Goldman is like a Rottweiler on a leash. The key is
bringing the handler, the Bank for International Settlements, under control.

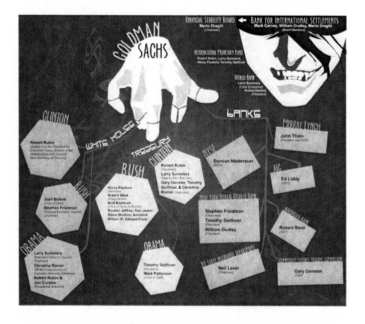

5

Preparing for the Money Meltdown

October 2009

I wrote my senator about the bailout.

The little one: Paulson and Bernanke's $700 billion donation to their favorite charity, Wall Street.

I urged her to rethink a commitment of nearly three-quarters of a trillion dollars of taxpayer money—my money and yours—when we had no way to pay it back other than going cap in hand to our friends in the Chinese Communist Party and Dubai to try to borrow it.

I say *try*, because for years Congress has been spending hundreds of billions of dollars a year more than it takes in and our Marxist and Muslim bankers are getting more than a little skeptical about whether we will ever be able to repay them.

No wonder. We are currently in debt more than $11 trillion, and this is just the government IOUs like Treasury bills and Treasury bonds.[1] Forget the money Congress has ripped off from the Social Security program and the tens of trillions more of unfunded liabilities (future financial commitments for which we do not have the money; estimates run to about $99 trillion).[2]

These numbers are so big they break the mind. It's hard to even fathom what they mean:

> If you laid one-dollar bills end to end, you could make a chain that stretches from Earth to the moon and back again two hundred times before you ran out of dollar bills! It would take a military jet flying at the speed of sound, reeling out a roll of dollar bills behind it, fourteen years before it reeled out one trillion dollar bills.[3]

You get the picture.

The interest on the national debt last year was $451,000,000,000. That's $1,235,616,438 a day, $51,484,018 an hour, $858,066 a minute, $14,301 a second.[4]

Makes you feel warm all over, doesn't it?

So I told my senator to knock it off.

She responded. She said that eighty-eight people had written in opposing the bail out and that five thousand had written in, in favor of it. But that this was a national crisis and she and the other members of Congress felt they were doing the right thing for the American people.

Arrogance doesn't even begin to say it.

These legislators, who have the financial IQ of roadkill, who have bankrupted our nation to the point of half a trillion dollars a year in interest for wars and welfare, know what's best for the American people?

The first bailout, which was a catastrophe, is of course, now being followed with a second that has more pork* than a Jimmy Dean sausage factory. This one is now branded as a "stimulus package" and is being muscled through Congress as I write this for a cool trillion and a quarter (including interest).[5]

You'd think someone had pumped LSD into the drinking water up there. With the new bailout-program-cum-stimulus-plan, the projected budget deficit for this year alone is about $1.8 trillion.

Where do they think they are going to get this money? Foreign central banks are dumping dollars like a bad habit, and U.S. debt is now about as welcome as an envelope of anthrax.

Which brings us to the point of this article, which is that when the government finishes their spending binge and wakes up to their eye-watering fiscal hangover, they will turn inward with a vengeance, seeking to filch money from every nook and cranny of the U.S. population.

---

*Pork—Short for pork-barrel politics; where a national politician arm-twists his fellows to get part of the national budget allocated to a pet project back home. For example, a local airport named in honor of the politician built at the cost of millions but which serves ten flights per day, mostly to and from Washington.

Tax Increases on the Wealthy

That there will be tax increases is a given. And they will start with the affluent. If you have worked hard and accumulated some wealth in the process, you are a high-profile target for higher taxes.

There is strong sentiment from the White House on down that if you make decent money, if you have accumulated some assets, the government should take part of it and spread it around.

Everyone is familiar with the president's statement to Joe the plumber during a campaign stop last October when he said, "I think when you spread the wealth around, it's good for everybody"—*everybody* being those people who didn't earn the money but who get some of yours.

But let's not quibble about who created the wealth; what's important is to spread it around, even things out.

And in case you're not mainlining MSNBC for your political news these days, you might have missed the fact that this point of view is not the sole province of the White House.

Some key members of Congress are very clear about their Das Kapitalian intentions.*

---

*Das Kapitalian—*Das Kapital* (1867) by Karl Marx, one of the founders of communism. Developed the idea of political economy as a point of social justice leading to the distribution of wealth.

Barney Frank, the chairman of the House Financial Services Committee, noted recently:

> "I think at this point there needs to be a focus on
> an immediate increase in spending, and I think
> this is a time when the deficit fear has to take a
> second seat.... I believe later on there should be tax
> increases. Speaking personally, I think there are
> a lot of rich people out there whom we can tax at
> a point down the road and recover some of this
> money."[6]

In fact, the good congressman may seek a shortcut to
your income. Instead of waiting for your tax return, your
salary itself could be at risk.

An article in *Financial Week* quotes the chairman of the
powerful Financial Services Committee as saying:

> Congress will consider legislation to extend some
> of the curbs on executive pay that now apply only
> to those banks receiving federal assistance.... The
> compensation restrictions would apply to all
> financial institutions and *might be extended to
> include all U.S. companies.*[7] [emphasis mine]

Channeling Karl Marx, Democratic Representative
James Moran, Frank's colleague in the House, had this to
say during a campaign stop:

"In the last several years, we have had the highest
corporate profit ever in American history . . .
but it hasn't been shared. And that's the problem.
Because we have been guided by a Republican
administration who believes in the simplistic
notion that people who have wealth are entitled to
keep it. And they have an antipathy toward the
means of redistributing wealth."[8]

Say what?

See, here's the scary part: he's serious. He is a United
States congressman on the Appropriations Committee—
one of the most important and powerful committees in
the House. He is also part of the Democratic leadership in
the House, and this man thinks there is something wrong
with people who consider that when they have accumulated
some assets they are entitled to keep them.

When you add gargantuan budget deficits to a government whose economic philosophy is grounded in a
craving to redistribute the wealth of its citizens, you
know they will be coming for those that have managed to
flourish and prosper.

Let's be blunt: if you earn well or you have assets, your
financial statement is at risk.

But the assault on your assets is not just coming from
potential changes in tax policy.

Confiscation of Personal Retirement Accounts

Testimony before the House Committee on Education and Labor in October 2008 suggested that personal retirement accounts (IRAs and 401[k]s) should be converted into government-controlled accounts called Guaranteed Retirement Accounts (GRAs).[9] They would be managed by that bastion of fiscal propriety the Social Security Administration.

The committee, chaired by California Democrat George Miller, heard the proposal from Teresa Ghilarducci, director of the Schwartz Center for Economic Policy Analysis at the New School for Social Research in New York. Her plan would eliminate tax breaks for 401(k) and similar retirement accounts such as IRAs and convert them into Guaranteed Retirement Accounts managed by the Social Security Administration.[10]

The Plan

Under Ghilarducci's plan, employees would have 5 percent of their pay mandatorily deducted from their pay and deposited into their GRA. This deduction would be in addition to Social Security and Medicare taxes, which would also have to continue being paid by employers.

The 5 percent would not be deductible by employers (as Social Security and Medicare taxes are), and only half of the

GRA assets could be passed along to your heirs at death. Presumably, Uncle would keep the other half.

"I'm just rearranging the breaks that are available now for 401(k)s and spreading the wealth," she said.[11]

There's that phrase again.

Argentina to Confiscate Retirement Plans

And just in case you think the idea of a government confiscating personal retirement accounts is out of the range of possibility, we urge you to read the story in the October 22, 2008, issue of the *Wall Street Journal*, which reported that the Argentinean government had seized all private pension and retirement accounts to fund government operations and a ballooning budget deficit.

Some articles note that this program was mandated by the president but still had to be approved by the Argentinean Congress, which is controlled by the president's Peronist political party.[12]

In reporting this possibility, I walk a tight line of trying not to be alarmist, yet not shying away from communicating the information that people should have about their savings, reserves, and investments.

In that regard, it is important to understand that there is no current legislation pending on this matter, and besides Ghilarducci's testimony, I have heard nothing formal that

I can substantiate which would validate that such a plan is imminent.

Still, the article dated October 21, 2008, by the widely respected Ambrose Evans-Pritchard, who writes for the UK *Telegraph,* is of interest:

Argentina seizes pension funds to pay debts. Who's next?

Here is a warning to us all. The Argentine state is taking control of the country's privately managed pension funds in a drastic move to raise cash.

Should we worry about our pensions?

It is a foretaste of what may happen across the world as governments discover that tax revenue, and discover that the bond markets are unwilling to plug the gap. The G-7* states are already acquiring an unhealthy taste for the arbitrary seizure of private property, I notice....

So, over $29 billion of Argentine civic savings are to be used as a funding kitty for the populist antics of President Cristina Kirchner. This has been dressed up as an anti-corruption and efficiency move. Aren't they always?...

---

*G-7—A group of finance ministers from the seven largest industrialized nations. No developing nations are allowed.

The funds being targeted are known as AFJPs or retirement accounts, but how long will it now be before Mrs. Kirchner cracks down on the entire $97 billion pool of private pensions? There are a lot of much-needed hard currency assets in those portfolios. . . .

President Kirchner has been eyeing the pension pool for some time. Last year she pushed through new rules forcing them to invest more money inside the country—always a warning signal.

My fear is that governments in the US, Britain, and Europe will display similar reflexes. Indeed, they have already done so. The forced-feeding of banks with fresh capital—whether they want it or not—and the seizure of the Fannie/Freddie mortgage giants before they were in fact in trouble (in order to prevent a Chinese buying strike of US bonds and prevent a spike in US mortgage rates), shows that private property can be co-opted—or eliminated—with little due process if that is required to serve the collective welfare. This is a slippery slope.[13] [emphasis mine]

Confiscation of Gold and Silver

But trillion-dollar budget deficits will require more.

Many turn to precious metals during times of economic duress. This is no surprise, as gold and silver have been a store of value for thousands of years and they have actual productive uses as opposed to paper currency, which has none other than its government-mandated use as money.

When a government has debased its currency at the printing press, it often takes measures to try to prevent its citizens from fleeing from the currency into precious metals or stronger currencies. One of the measures that has been used in the past is making the ownership of precious metals illegal. This seeks to stop the capital flight from its currency to hard assets.

Sound unreal?

We give you President Franklin D. Roosevelt on March 9, 1933:

> ... I, as President, do declare that ... the continued private hoarding of gold and silver by subjects of the United States poses a grave threat to the peace, equal justice, and well-being of the United States; and that appropriate measures must be taken immediately to protect the interests of our people.
>
> Therefore ... I hereby proclaim that such gold and silver holdings are prohibited, and that all such

coin, bullion, or other possessions of gold and
silver be tendered within fourteen days to agents of
the Government of the United States for compensation at the official price....

All safe deposit boxes in banks or financial institutions have been sealed....

Therefore be advised that your vault box must
remain sealed, and may only be opened in the
presence of an agent of the Internal Revenue
Service.[14]

It may surprise you to know that laws still exist that
give the president the authority to prohibit the ownership
of gold, silver, and other assets during emergencies. The
Trading with the Enemy Act and the International
Emergency Economic Powers Act can be used to freeze
privately held assets and prohibit their possession anytime
the president issues a proclamation of emergency.

Currency Controls

Currency controls are yet another way governments try to
contain the adverse effects of printing too much money.

Wikipedia defines it this way: "Currency control is a
system whereby a country tries to regulate the value of
money (currency) within its borders."[15]

This can take many forms, but for our purposes, one of the ways governments implement currency controls is to limit or prevent assets from leaving the country. You might not be able to move money or other assets abroad (as that would take them out of the grasp of Uncle). Converting dollars into a stronger currency could become illegal, as could transferring funds out of the country to buy gold, if it were outlawed here.

Increased taxes, currency controls, and outlawing the ownership of precious metals are just some of the potential consequences that could emanate from a government that will soon wake from a spending binge the likes of which has never been seen before. And when the enormity of the damage they will have created starts to dawn on them and starts to dawn on the rest of the country, threatening their House or Senate seats, they will turn on the wealthy like machines from *The Matrix*, seeking income for the government in ways that all such governments have done in ages past—ways we have detailed above.

It is difficult to say it more succinctly or bluntly than was done in the highly regarded *Casey Report* earlier this year:

> Your government considers you a national resource
> to be exploited. If you don't get your money out of
> the country before the government gets your

money out of you, you're an idiot, and you're going to get what you deserve.[16]

As the U.S. government deficits continue to roll forward and tax revenues continue to fall, it is a foregone conclusion that not only will taxes rise (forget the president's campaign promises; the idea that you can drive the government into more than a trillion dollars of debt every year and not raise taxes is a cruel joke) but the government will also seek new and "clever" ways to come after your assets.

You may blow this off as alarmist, conspiratorial, or just plain wrong. But, without getting dramatic or overly "serious" here, I suggest that you ignore this data at your own peril.

Suggestions on what to do about this situation, both personally and politically, are detailed in the next and final article.

6

The Financial Crisis:
What You Can Do About It

November 2009

I have said it a number of times that there has been a *coup d'état.*

I'm not talking about Honduras. I'm talking about Wall Street, London, and Basel, Switzerland, and the fact that we are in the midst of a global financial coup instigated by a *Clockwork Orange* gang of international bankers.

The economic bloodletting has abated for now—at least the media's promotion of it has. In its place the media fawns on the very people who caused this crisis as they move forward to secure total global economic control. The carefully orchestrated spin is now designed to create acceptance of their "restructuring" of the international financial system in order to ensure this can never happen again.

Yes, I know, it sounds like an outtake from *Conspiracy Theory*, but I'm not Mel Gibson and you're not Julia Roberts. And this is not a screenplay.

Whether or not you accept the idea that the financial crisis was created for the purpose of replacing the United States and the U.S. dollar as the stable point in international finance with a global financial dictator and a new world currency, this scenario—set forth in our prior articles—is now in full swing.

This from the G-20 meeting in Pittsburgh September 26, 2009:

G-20 leaders push global economic reforms Friday

PITTSBURGH —

... The Pittsburgh meeting marked the third G-20 leaders summit in less than a year as the countries continued to grapple with a debilitating downturn that has resulted in millions of unemployed around the world, the loss of trillions of dollars in wealth and massive amounts of government stimulus spending designed to jump-start economic growth....

"We are not going to walk away from the greatest economic crisis since the Great Depression and leave unchanged and leave in place the tragic vulnerabilities that caused this crisis," Treasury Secretary Timothy Geithner told reporters....

Geithner said the G-20 countries had reached a consensus on the "basic outline" of a proposal to limit bankers' compensation by the end of this year. *He said it would involve setting separate standards in each of the countries and would be overseen by the Financial Stability Board, an international group of central bankers, finance ministers and regulators that has representation from all the G-20 nations.*[1] [emphasis mine]

While Geithner & Company are quietly empowering the Financial Stability Board (FSB), the United States and every other industrialized nation on earth are gushing money into their economies as if the printing presses were broken water mains.

The SDR

And just to make sure the planet drowns in the stuff, the International Monetary Fund (IMF) just announced (September 2009) that they had created $250 billion worth of SDRs and are going to spread them around the planet like a monetary Johnny Appleseed.[2]

SDR stands for "Special Drawing Rights." This is a currency that has been created by the IMF out of . . . eh . . . thin air. They say it is money and it is.

The SDR is "backed" by the dollar and the euro.
These, in turn, are backed by . . . the same thin air. The
IMF can create the stuff in unlimited quantities with
digital alchemy, which amounts to simply adding zeros
on a computer screen to suit the appetites of those
countries dining at the IMF's table.

The CIA

But here's an interesting little secret: it wasn't really the IMF
that created SDRs. A recently declassified CIA document
makes clear that the fiscal geniuses at Langley did. In a
secretly classified memo dated December 9, 1965, the
agency discusses manipulating the gold market with
central banks and the need for more "liquidity" because of
the dollar's perceived weakness at the time. A section of the
memo is quoted here. Take special note of the last sentence.

SECRET

Increasing liquidity

*Trade won't be able to grow, and the system will
remain vulnerable to speculation unless there is
regular growth in the international money supply.*

*Gold can't provide the needed increase: industrial
and speculative demand is too high. U.S. payment
deficits can't either: foreigners are unwilling to hold*

more dollars when we run large deficits and unable to increase net reserves by accumulating dollars when our deficits are small.

Our strategy is to supplement gold and dollars with a new international asset, Special Drawing Rights (SDR).[3] [emphasis mine]

There were too many dollars in circulation and foreign governments that were holding dollars in reserve were considering turning theirs in for gold at the time. The CIA was trying to head off a run on Fort Knox by foreign governments.

Nixon Slams the Gold Window Shut

You see, until 1971, the U.S. dollar was pegged to gold at $35 an ounce. In other words, any foreign government (but not U.S. citizens) could turn their dollars in for gold—every $35 would get them an ounce of gold. When the costs of the Korean War and the Vietnam War turned our economy into a debtor nation (having to borrow to pay bills), we printed more dollars than there was gold to cover them.[4] Other nations knew this and grew concerned about their ability to receive gold in exchange for their dollars. In fact, French president Charles de Gaulle started cashing in France's greenbacks for the real deal.

To head off a run on our bullion, in 1971 Richard Nixon closed the "gold window."[5]

Without the dollar being tied to a physical commodity, the Federal Reserve Bank had free license to print away.

As you know by now, the Federal Reserve Bank is a private corporation. The shareholders of the Fed are the large multinational banks, many of which are head-quartered in New York.

The Fed's real purpose is to create money in order to lend it to the United States government. Given that it is a private corporation, the Fed's money is basically a corporate currency. At its core, it's no different than if Microsoft started to print bank notes that Congress designated as legal tender for the exchange of goods and services.

Think about that; it's corporate money. Pull a $5 bill out of your pocket/purse and you will see that it is labeled "Federal Reserve Note."

When the government spends more than it takes in, it must borrow the difference. The Fed prints up dead presidents and lends them to Sam (it's mostly digital money these days). And, of course, they charge interest on the money they loan, so it is in their interest for the country to spend more than it takes in.

Wars and Deficits

One of the primary reasons that a country goes in debt is to finance a war. Wars are costly. They create deficits, which require borrowing—from the Fed.

If there isn't a war, someone can simply start one.

March 10, 1964:

A secretly installed White House tape recorder is running.

President Johnson is on the phone with Secretary of Defense Robert McNamara regarding Vietnam:

"We need somebody over there that can get us some better plans than we got....

"What I want is somebody that can lay up some plans to trap these guys . . . and whoop the hell out of 'em. Kill some of 'em. That's what I want to do."

McNamara:

"I'll try to bring something back that will meet that objective."[6]

August 4, 1964:

President Johnson goes before Congress claiming that U.S. ships have been attacked in the Gulf of Tonkin by North Vietnamese gunships. He seeks a joint resolution from Congress expressing support for all necessary action to protect our armed forces and to assist the nations in the region.[7]

On August 7, 1964, Congress passes joint resolution H.J. RES 1145, the Gulf of Tonkin Resolution, which gives President Johnson blanket authority to increase U.S. involvement in the war between North and South Vietnam.

Johnson and McNamara unleash the dogs of war.

Dogs which cost the government $200 billion in 1974 dollars ($686 billion in 2008 dollars).

McNamara and the National Security Agency later admit that no such attack in the Gulf of Tonkin ever occurred.[8]

Isn't that special?

Now why in the world would the government create a war that didn't exist? I mean, who would benefit from such a thing?

Not American servicemen, fifty-eight thousand of whom lost their lives. Not America itself—the war tore the country apart. Not the Vietnamese people, 1.4 million of whom died, many incinerated by napalm. (We love you, Bob.)

But the owners of the Fed, the New York bankers who are always willing to, you know, extend a helping hand and lend some of their monopoly money to a needy Uncle—these guys got bloody rich when the government had to borrow billions to finance the war.

The outstanding national debt of the United States is about $13 trillion as of the writing of this book. The Fed doesn't own it all: China and Japan have some, as do others. The government pays out $452,000,000—half a trillion—a year in interest on the national debt. They get the money to pay the interest (and other expenses such as war and welfare) from income taxes made possible by the Sixteenth Amendment.

This is what my old man would have called "a killer deal."

Fiat Currencies

For the last several years, budget deficits (shortfalls) have been running a few hundred billion a year. Not good. But this year (2009), the deficit (outgo over income) will be $1.4 trillion. That means that the Fed's printing presses are burning rubber. In addition to the U.S., virtually every industrial nation on earth has gone to the presses in some fanatical jihad of liquidity.

What does this mean—with the IMF printing up $250 billion of SDRs and the governments of the world having their own fiat printing parties? It means that currencies are going to get less valuable and commodities will become more valuable.

Here is a definition of *fiat currency*. (I have taken *Wikipedia*'s definition and edited it for simplicity and am solely responsible for the content.)

Fiat money is money declared by a government to be legal tender. The term derives from the Latin *fiat*, meaning "let it be done." Fiat money achieves value because a government accepts it in payment of taxes and says it can be used within the country as a "tender" (offering) to pay all debts. In effect, this allows it to be used to buy goods and services and to pay tax. Where fiat money is used as currency, the term *fiat currency* is used. The most widely held reserve currency, the U.S. dollar, is a fiat currency, as are other widely held currencies like the euro, pound sterling, and the yen.

In short, fiat currency is paper money sanctioned by a government. What stands behind the currency is the "full faith and credit" of the government, not gold or silver or any physical goods or services.

All of which leads us to the question, what does one do when fiat currencies are spreading like a plague of locusts?

When the government finishes their spending binge and wakes up to their eye-watering fiscal hangover, they will turn inward with a vengeance, seeking to filch money from every nook and cranny of the U.S. population.

When they do that, you need to be prepared. The following are my suggestions. They are based on thirty years of working in the area of banking, finance, credit, and investment. Yet they are no more or less than my opinions. I have no crystal ball and offer no guarantees. What I do offer is the best advice I can, based on the data I have to hand.

Solutions

That said, here goes.

Precious Metals

When fiat currencies are debased, people turn to precious metals.

Why?

For one, they have intrinsic value. There is something almost magical about them. They have been prized and admired by people the world over for thousands of years. They have been used for everything from jewelry and crowns to tombs and offerings to the gods—a gold band symbolizes a marriage and pharaohs were buried in gold coffins. In modern day, both gold and silver have commercial and industrial uses.

And both have been used as money for eons. In 700 BC, Mesopotamian merchants used silver as a form of exchange. The Greek drachma, the Roman denarius and the British pound sterling all used silver in the creation of their money. Gold, too, was used to coin money hundreds of years before the time of Christ. Its use as the primary medium of monetary exchange has carried forward through time well into the twentieth century.

It was in 1933 that the U.S. government banned the ownership of gold. Still, dimes, quarters, and halves contained 90 percent silver up until 1964, after which time the government ceased the practice.

Both metals also have extensive commercial and industrial uses: silver in photography, batteries, electronics, solar energy, and water purification, to name a few. Gold is used in nanotechnology, electronics, dentistry, rocket engines, as well as watches and pens, to name a few more.

In short, man's fascination with gold and silver's decorative applications, their more recent industrial applications, as well as their use as money dates back thousands of years and is not about to change.

So when things get unstable in the world of finance, when fiat currencies are pouring off the presses in a blizzard of fiscal confetti, people turn to precious metals—gold and silver (and, to a lesser degree, platinum).

I have promoted the ownership of gold and silver since gold was under $300 an ounce and silver was $4.00 an ounce. As I write this, they are currently trading at $1,046 and $17.57, respectively.

These are handsome appreciations over a period of a few years, and there are those who believe gold and silver have run their course. I just finished reading a newsletter by one prognosticator who is convinced that the bull market* in precious metals is over. Perhaps he's right. Those who think the bull market in precious

---

*Bull market—A financial market in which prices are rising and are expected to keep rising.

metals has run its course use government statistics to show that inflation is under control. But no one falsifies statistics like politicians. Even if the figures are correct, I think these metals markets have a long way to run.

Governments are still spraying dollars (or pounds or yen or yuan or euros) into their economies like some fiscal Agent Orange. And the IMF is engaged in distributing its SDR party favors cited above.

Inflation and Deflation

When the amount of money in circulation exceeds the goods and services available, the result is an economic illness called inflation.

Inflation is simply more money in circulation than there are goods and services to purchase. The money "competes" for the goods.

If you were, say, in a classroom and you had an orange to sell and every kid in the class had $10, the money would "compete" for the purchase of the orange, which would probably sell for $10.

But what if every kid in the classroom had $100? What would happen to the price of the orange?

This is called inflation.

Deflation is just the opposite. What if the kids in our classroom each had a buck?

This is not the rocket science that Harvard Business School professors would have you believe.

So with the amount of money in circulation reaching stratospheric levels (see following chart), why is the consumer price index hibernating like a grizzly in February?

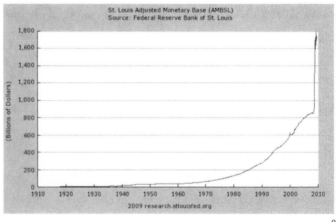

9

The answer comes from Nobel Laureate Milton Friedman who, in 1972, found that there was a lag of over a year before an expanded money supply caused a noticeable effect on inflation and interest rates.[10] This is supported in a recent study by two economists at the Bank of England—Nicoletta Batini and Edward Nelson—who analyzed U.S. and UK money growth rates, inflation, and interest rates from 1953 to 2001.[11]

They found the same correlation. Another study at the European Central Bank documented an eighteen-month lag.

The U.S. government started pouring money into the economy in the fourth quarter of 2008 and is continuing to do so. The Europeans followed a bit later. All of which is to say that if Friedman and the others are correct, inflation should become manifest around the summer of 2010.

For all of the above reasons, I recommend that people place some of their reserve assets into precious metals. My recommendation is that 20 –25 percent be in precious metals—for the adventurous, even more.

There is no magic to this figure. Some people will be comfortable with a smaller percentage; others will do more. But having some assets in gold and silver in times like these is something with which Yoda would agree.

What to Buy?

Silver

I favor silver. I recommend an allocation of about 70 percent silver, 30 percent gold. There are several reasons for this. First of all, it's cheaper. If you had $10,000 to invest today, you could buy 569 ounces of silver, but only 10 ounces of gold (9½ really). Now of course gold moves (appreciates and depreciates) in dollars and silver in cents, but let's look at a little history.

When gold hit its peak thirty years ago, it topped out at $850 an ounce. Today, it is trading at about $1,050.

When gold hit $850, silver peaked at $50 an ounce. But today, silver is trading a bit over $17. You think it may have some room to the upside?

There are other factors involved, but the bottom line is, I think you have much better upside potential with silver.

Silver can be purchased in a number of different forms. If you are buying silver strictly for investment purposes, with no thought to the use of silver for money or exchange, then one can buy bullion in 10 oz, 100 oz, or 1,000 oz bars.

Junk Silver

The breakdown of the silver would depend on how much one has to spend. If you have $12,000 (given today's prices) I would recommend a bag of "junk" silver. Junk silver is pre-1965 dimes, quarters, and halves.

Silver coins prior to 1965 were made from 90 percent silver. So they appreciate with the silver market and are legal currency of the United States. They protect against inflation and serve as a potential source of currency if the financial system and/or the economy completely collapse.

If you have a few hundred thousand to invest, get two or three bags.

Silver Eagles

Several governments mint gold and silver coins. In addition to the United States—Canada, Australia, China, Mexico, and Austria are well-known manufacturers of such coins.

Buying one-ounce silver coins is an excellent second tier to one's silver portfolio. I recommend that you buy the one-ounce silver coin of the country in which you live if they mint one.

If you live in America, the name of the one-ounce coin minted by the U.S. government is the Silver Eagle. These are not official currency—they aren't government-sanctioned money. But in hard times, they would very likely serve as an excellent medium of exchange.

Silver Eagles normally sell for about 10 percent over the spot price* of silver. As I write this, Silver Eagles are selling for about $18 a piece. So, 1,000 Eagles would be $18,000—and so forth.

There are also local and regional companies that mint one-ounce silver coins. They are almost always priced for less than the Eagles. This simply has to do with the trust factor. If you had to exchange a couple of silver

---

*Spot price—The price that is quoted if you want to buy any commodity today.

coins for a tank of gas, the coins minted by the U.S. government are more likely to be accepted than those from a local mint.

Given this fact, it makes sense to pay the slight premium for the coins minted by the government.

The third part of the silver portfolio should be silver bars. Again, the amount depends on how much you are intending to invest, but 99 percent pure silver bars are sold in 10 oz, 100 oz, and 1,000 oz sizes.

These are called bullion bars and tend to be purchased more for the purpose of straight investment than the ability to use them in times of economic crisis.

Gold

Like silver, gold bullion can be purchased in the form of bars and coins. Both are sold in multiple sizes. For instance, gold coins are sold in 1 oz, ½ oz, ¼ oz, and 1/10 oz. While there is a premium for the smaller-sized coins (and the premium is usually higher the smaller the size), I recommend having some of these smaller sizes in your portfolio.

The reason is, if things get financially chaotic—I'm not saying they will, but it is not out of the question—then having some smaller denominations can provide a better medium of exchange. In other words, it would be easier to, say, pay for the family's groceries using a

1/10 oz gold coin (currently $142) than a 1 oz coin (currently $1,143).

One-ounce gold coins are the most common and are frequently traded. Gold bars come in a wide variety of sizes: 1 oz, 10 oz, 100 oz, 400 oz, and more.

Again, I recommend some fractional gold coins for potential use for trade and barter in case things become financially chaotic. In times such as those, fiat currency becomes essentially worthless and gold and silver coins become "the coin of the realm."

Model Portfolio

Here's an example of a "model portfolio," if someone had $100,000 to invest in precious metals today. I use that figure because it is round. If you have less to invest (or more), you can proportion it accordingly. This portfolio is at today's prices and the price of metals will almost certainly be different when you are reading this book.

Moreover, these recommendations are not set in stone. They are simply how I look at these markets. Many people favor gold more strongly than I do, while others are not interested in coins and prefer bullion bars, which they buy strictly for investment purposes.

To repeat, I place considerable value on gold and silver coins as potential backup "currency" should the wheels totally come off the economic wagon.

That said, I feel this kind of allotment would serve people well using the $100,000 model.

2 bags of "junk" silver	$ 26,000
750 Silver Eagles	$ 14,798
50 x 10 oz silver bars	$ 9,200
10 x 100 oz silver bars	$ 18,330
Total silver	$ 68,328
10 x 1/10 oz gold coins	$ 1,410
10 x ¼ oz gold coins	$ 2,900
9 x ½ oz gold coins	$ 5,193
10 x 1 oz Gold Eagles	$ 11,410
1 x 10 oz gold bar	$ 10,662
Total gold	$ 31,575
Total	$ 99,903

Leaving you a few bucks for shipping.

Where to Buy?

It is a sign of the times that there seem to be more precious metals dealers than car dealerships these days. So there is no shortage of places to shop for your precious metals.

I use the word *shop* advisedly because precious metals prices can vary widely. Dealers usually charge a certain percent over the spot price of the metal for coins or bars. This percentage varies from dealer to dealer. The big houses tend to be competitive, but there is no guarantee of that.

The markup from the spot price can run from 3 percent to 4.5 percent on a single Gold Eagle to 11 percent plus for a single Silver Eagle. And these are just ballpark numbers taken from a few key sites. Moreover, these percentages diminish rapidly as the volume and the amount of the purchase increase.

The bottom line is you need to shop the pricing. And in doing so, you need to contact the prospective dealers on the same day to get comparative pricing. Precious metals markets can move by the minute. However, dealers generally lock in prices for one trading day (though not always, so be sure to check).

And while price is always important, there are other factors involved— the foremost of which is to deal with a well-established, trusted precious metals dealer. Many of the top firms have been around for decades. It is hard to stay in business that long, particularly in the precious metals business, if you are not honest and trustworthy. Length of time in business is certainly not a guarantee, but it is a good gauge.

You also want to make sure, if you have the metals shipped, that the package is insured, and if they charge for shipping, how much.

I use Colorado Gold for myself and my clients (www.coloradogold.com) 1-888-786-8822. The owner's name is Don Stott, who has been a precious metals broker for more than thirty years. I have found him to be trustworthy in all of my dealings with him.

Moreover, he has the best prices for precious metals that I can find. This doesn't mean you couldn't search and find someone lower. This isn't a "price guarantee" for Colorado Gold. It is just a statement of my experience. Don charges 1.5 percent for his brokerage services. For orders over $35,000 he charges 1 percent including insured shipping, and ¾ percent including insured shipping for orders over $75,000.

Storage

There are several ways to buy and store precious metals.

The first is to have the metals shipped to your home and put in a safe. Even if the order is too large for home delivery, I recommend that you take delivery of some gold and silver coins, as these take up very little room and it may be important to have them close to hand at some point.

If you are only going to take partial delivery of the order and want the rest stored, then you need a facility that specializes in precious metals storage—not your bank safe-deposit box, as "bank holidays" (banks closing for some period of time) are a very real prospect for the financial industry in the United States in the years to come. I would not recommend storing your metals with your dealer. That is asking for trouble.

Some of the larger precious metals dealers have relationships to which they can refer you or deliver your metals. Needless to say, the selection of a company to store your metals is extremely important. Ideally, you should go and physically inspect the facility.

If your dealer does not provide you with a referral, you have to find one. I know that Brinks offers precious metals storage at some of its locations. But the best place for storage appears to be a facility in Delaware called Delaware Depository.

Delaware Depository

I have not used them nor have I been there, so please do your own due diligence on any metals storage facility you are considering. However, from the looks of their services and their licensing, they appear to be an excellent choice (www.delawaredepository.com).

There are a couple of other options that are worthy of mention.

GoldMoney

One is GoldMoney (www.goldmoney.com).

This is from their website:

> GoldMoney® enables you to hold gold, silver & platinum that is fully insured and stored securely in specialised bullion vaults in Zurich and London. All metal is owned directly by you with no counterparty risk!

I have yet to personally use them, though multiple people have recommended them. They provide some unique services. Go to the site and check them out.

Perth Mint

Another alternative if you do not want to store your metals at home is The Perth Mint (www.perthmint.com). The Perth Mint was founded in 1899 and is owned by the government of Western Australia. They have a unique, highly regarded program of storing precious metals that you buy from them and providing you with a widely recognized "Perth Mint Certificate." The mint has a handful of dealers in key jurisdictions around the world.

This brief summary is from their website:

> The Perth Mint has a strong reputation for excellence and innovation and now offers a variety of different methods of precious metal investment to cater for individual investor needs.
>
> Investors who do not want the inconvenience and risk of storing their precious metals can take advantage of the investment products that The Perth Mint has developed. These products allow investors to buy gold, silver and platinum via its Certificate and Depository programs....
>
> Alternatively, The Perth Mint manufactures a wide range of bullion coins and bullion bars for those who prefer to store physical precious metal themselves. Information on these products can be accessed by clicking on any one of the four menu choices above. If you have any questions about The Perth Mint's investment products or how to invest in gold, silver and platinum, please contact us.

Check it out. The Perth Mint is one of the world's most enduring institutions of precious metals.

In short, you can buy yourself a good safe and take personal delivery of your metals; you can have your metals stored at a professional precious metals storage facility; you can purchase from and have your metals stored in a place like The Perth Mint, or any combination thereof.

Foreign Currencies

Remember, no national currency is backed by gold today. The strength of a currency, then, is really a reflection of the economic health and productivity of the country issuing it. The dollar's swan dive over the last couple of years is a reflection of America's massive budget deficits, trade imbalances, and the corresponding fall from economic grace. There was at time, not so long ago, when the American economy was the envy of the world and the greenback was "as good as gold."

This is no longer the case.

The strongest major economy on the planet today is that of the PRC—People's Republic of China. And this is why I recommend diversifying some of one's assets into the yuan (also referred to as the renminbi or RMB). Am I a fan of the government of mainland China? I am not. But in one of the great demonstrations of political-economic irony, the commissars at the Chinese Communist Party have turned the Chinese economy into a quasi–free market system that is now the most productive on the planet. Go figure. But that productivity provides an underlying natural strength to the yuan.

Make no mistake. China has been hurt by the global depression. But this has been like Ray Robinson landing a punishing uppercut to Jake "Raging Bull" LaMotta in the final round of their last encounter (Sugar Ray won four of the five in what are arguably the greatest middleweight fights of all time; Robinson landed a hail of punches in the last round, but LaMotta never went down), not like Buster Douglas's historic knockout of "Iron Mike" Tyson in Tokyo in 1990.

And if you are not a fight fan or find the boxing metaphors on the far side of tortured, I think you get the picture: China has taken a hit, but it is still on its feet and producing, while the finance ministers of the rest of the world's economies gather at G-20 meetings and dine on platitudes while issuing pretentious calls for "quantitative easing" (means print more money).

Yuan/RMB deposit accounts can be opened at Ever-Bank. EverBank (www.everbank.com) is a bank head-quartered in Florida. They take deposits in U.S. dollars but you can also open accounts in several foreign currencies. This enables you to diversify some assets into other currencies that hopefully will stand up more strongly than the dollar.

This bank's deposits, even those in foreign currencies, are insured by the U.S. government for $250,000 per account holder. (Note: This insurance was increased from $100,000 to $250,000 last year but is set to revert to $100,000 on January 1, 2014. This lowering of coverage does not apply to IRAs and other certain retirement accounts, which will remain at $250,000 per depositor.)

However, if you are married, you can actually get coverage for up to $1,000,000. Here's how.

You open an account in your name. It is covered for $250,000. Your spouse opens an account is his/her name. It is covered for $250,000. You open a joint account in both names and each of you is covered for an additional $250,000.[12]

For further currency diversification and to protect against a declining dollar, one could consider the Norwegian krone. Yes, I know, it's probably not sitting at the top of your investment radar screen. But these folks run one of the most fiscally responsible governments on the planet. Many do not know that Norway is the third largest exporter of oil on the planet (tons of the stuff off their coast in the North Sea) and utilizes its $1.5 billion a week in oil revenues to keep this country as economically strong as their Viking ancestors.

The *Chicago Tribune* reported on this phenomenon in November 2007:

> OSLO, Norway — If you wanted to design a small, 21st-century nation from scratch, combining outrageous good fortune with virtue, you'd probably come up with something like Norway.
>
> With a per capita income of $65,509, Norway ranks second only to super-rich Luxembourg. Much of the wealth derives from North Sea oil, but Norwegians have barely touched a penny of it, instead putting more than $350 billion into an investment fund for future generations.[13]

Norway numbers:

Per capita income: $65,509 (second only to Luxembourg)

Healthcare services: Available to all of its 4.6 million people, with the cap on out-of-pocket expenses at $200 a year.

Maternity leave: Working women get a year off at 80 percent pay.

Oil exports: The world's third largest after Saudi Arabia and Russia. Its 2.9 million barrels a day bring in roughly $1.8 billion a week (at $96 a barrel).[14]

Norway has a 10 percent budget *surplus*. This compared to the 40 percent, $1.4 trillion budget *deficit* in the U.S. But that is just the beginning because the fiscal brain trust in the White House and Congress is now calling for a "second stimulus"—a trillion-dollar healthcare plan and multibillion-dollar extensions of unemployment insurance.

These people are smoking something. The country is in the midst of an economic meltdown and they're like . . .

Nancy to Harry:
"Dude, I know, let's keep paying people not to work."

Harry:
"Awesome. Let me check with the O man, but I know he'll be down with this."

For whatever reason, the government of Norway is not afflicted by BDD—budget deficit disorder—the inability to spend less than you take in. All of which is to say that the Norwegian krone is backed by hundreds of billions a year in oil revenue and that rarest of organizations, a fiscally responsible government.

Krone deposits are also available at EverBank.

An Offshore Solution

Growing numbers of people are moving assets offshore into gold, silver, and stronger currencies such as the Norwegian krone and the Chinese yuan. Seeing the coming tsunami of government debt and inflation and potential confiscation of personal wealth, many are turning to offshore jurisdictions that provide privacy and outstanding asset protection.

Government taxing authorities would love to have people believe that moving assets offshore is somehow immoral or even illegal. Nothing could be further from the truth.

According to the U.S. Government Accountability Office, eighty-three of the nation's one hundred largest corporations, including world-class brands such as General Motors, Pepsi, News Corp, and Wells Fargo, had subsidiaries in offshore tax havens in 2007. In fact, hundreds of thousands of offshore entities—corporations and foundations—operate legally in tax haven jurisdictions from Panama to Liechtenstein, from the British Virgin Islands (BVI) to Hong Kong.

Offshore corporations, foundations, and trusts can usually be set up for nominal amounts and enable those creating them to move some of their assets out of dollars and out of the reach of fiscally irresponsible, avaricious governments. Offshore entities not only enable those creating them to protect their assets from the world's most litigious society but also give them access to world markets that are not available in the United States. Offshore entities also can help facilitate the movement of currency or capital should the U.S. impose currency controls or seek to confiscate precious metals holdings.

There are many companies that provide these services. However, I decided to research this area myself. After considerable study and enough international travel to make my air miles account pregnant with upgrades, I set up a site to help people who were considering this strategy at www.offshorefinancialsolutions.com.

Some words of caution: Do not set up an offshore entity to evade taxes. It is against the law. Panamanian foundations, for instance, are terrific for asset protection; they are wonderful estate planning tools, and they provide access to foreign currency, securities, and commodities markets.

But these activities should be undertaken to protect your assets and give you access to foreign investment markets and freedom of movement of your capital—not for tax evasion. U.S. citizens are required to report offshore accounts and income they earn from anywhere in the world, so our strongest possible advice is that you obey the laws of your country regarding tax matters.

That said, there are some select legal tax advantages in conducting business offshore. To understand the tax rules for conducting business or investment activities offshore, you should have the advice of a top offshore tax accountant. One CPA who specializes in this area is Vernon Jacobs. His website is www.vernonjacobs.com. He offers offshore tax advice to other CPAs, lawyers, and individuals, as well as access to several books he has written on the subject.

You should also be aware that if you open up offshore accounts (e.g., deposit accounts, brokerage accounts) you must report their existence on your federal income tax return. One of Vernon Jacobs's books covers this topic in considerable detail.

But regardless of where you might have this done, bear in mind that Uncle is broke. He's more than broke; he's short more than a trillion this year with projections for the same well into the future, and I think you would be wise to consider moving some of your assets offshore and out of U.S. dollars.

Summary

Financial Solutions

In summary, we recommend the following, as long as you bear in mind that conditions change and markets change. And while these recommendations are based on the best advice I can provide, they are also based on current conditions and prevailing market factors. That said,

1. approximately 25 percent of your reserves should be placed in precious metals;
2. about 70 percent of those metals should be in silver and 30 percent in gold;
3. another 10–15 percent should be placed in foreign currencies—specifically, the Chinese yuan (RMB) and the Norwegian krone;
4. the balance should be kept liquid in cash and short-term Treasury bills so that you can take advantage of opportunities that will become available as economies continue to deteriorate.

Political Solutions

Political solutions are detailed in the first two articles, "Behind the Wizard's Curtain" and "Hitler's Bank Goes Global," but I want to reiterate and expand upon them here one last time. Because if we are ever going to truly take control of global financial matters in a way that benefits people and not bankers, there are two vital things that need to be done.

One

In the short term, members of Congress and members of the Parliaments of the G-20 nations should insist that a representative legislative body be set up at international level that has full oversight and corrective powers over the FSB and similar international financial and trade organizations. This would automatically ensure that national central banks would be subject to the full oversight and corrective powers of duly constituted legislative bodies.

In the U.S. a body like the FSB must be confirmed either by treaty or congressional-executive agreement (though they seem unaware of this fact as of this writing). This treaty or congressional-executive agreement would serve as a vehicle to create a legislative oversight and enforcement body over the FSB.

In the case of inaction by the executive branch (which has been the case to date), this may require the introduction of formal legislation. I outline how to do that in "Hitler's Bank Goes Global."

It is important to note here that other member countries have similar mechanisms. Now, more than ever, citizens must start paying close attention to the

machinations of unelected international financial bodies
or they will find themselves operating at the effect of such
bodies with no real remedy to hand.

Challenging to be sure, but the alternative opens the
door to an Orwellian world that has no place for the
exercise of individual liberty. On the other hand, creating
this structure will help guarantee personal freedom for
all people.

Two

Once that is done, the creation of an international
monetary system that is based on property and production would have to be insisted upon.

In other words, a monetary system that is not based
on fiat money or an unworkable commodity, such as
gold, but on what money actually represents, and that is
all of the production (goods and services) and property
value (real estate and land value) of nations.

For example, a realistic assessment of the country's
gross domestic product (GDP) and property value
would yield an amount—say $100 billion. The country's
national bank would ensure that was the amount of
currency in circulation. They couldn't print more or less
than that amount, and that would mean no inflation, no
deflation, just sufficient money to buy what was available
to buy.

This would guarantee that the economy is based on stable and real economic measures. It would be based on the most fundamental definitions of inflation and deflation—inflation being the result of more money than goods, and deflation being more goods than money—and financial matters would be maintained accordingly.

Based on this system each state or country would be allocated, as its money, the exact value of its property, real or personal, as well as its current value of production. The currency would be issued by an international body, which could be the IMF, but only once it is irrevocably and unalterably under the oversight and corrective powers of a legislative body and bound by this monetary system, precluding private, corporate, and political abuse.

In other words, all branches of government would be bound by the formula described above and, thus, neither the executive or legislative branch nor any banking organization could institute policies that are debt based.

Once in place, each year, by careful survey, the extant funds in a country or state would be increased or decreased to match its productivity on the premise that money must exist to purchase that which exists to be purchased.

This would make the pursuit of happiness a reality for all people and make the American dream a global reality.

This would result in actual free trade and resolve balance of payment problems, as the currencies would be interchangeable, all having the same value. Free trade would also include free trade of oil. It would allow for oil exploration that is unfettered by unsustainable monetary policy. It would end currency manipulation and artificial oil scarcity, eliminating the most prevalent cause for current wars, which aside from human death and misery create considerable environmental damage. It would also, obviously, abolish carbon credits. In short, it would create an abundance of energy and a future of productivity in which all life would be able to prosper.

I don't take pleasure or joy in detailing the economic takeover of the planet by a gang of pinstriped hoods. But these are not normal times, and if one is informed, he can take the appropriate steps to protect himself and his family and what assets he may have put away for the proverbial rainy day.

I hope you find these suggestions helpful. And remember to keep your powder dry.

7
2012 Act Three Update Introduction

As with the original publication of *Crisis by Design*, I continued to follow the global financial crisis as it moved to Europe – and wrote about it.

There are two articles that make up this updated version. The first exposes how Goldman Sachs helped Greece deceive the European Central Bank about its toxic debt structure.

It also turns a spot light on the one quadrillion dollars of derivatives that are, to use a Buffetism, financial weapons of mass destruction.

The second article examines the media's tactical flanking of the current European financial crisis for the IMF and Bank for International Settlements. What's going on in Europe is the second act of a staged play.

The articles were written several months apart, but both should be viewed as a tightening of the noose around the throat of the global financial system.

It is a personal fixation of mine that governments strike me as heroin addicts. Civilizations can crumble before their very eyes and they continue to spend and borrow in acts of political and cultural suicide. So forgive me, or not, the fact that I repeat the metaphor in both articles – it's just too apt. You will also find a call at the end of each article for a currency based on products and property – real things. Radical, I know, but it works.

Keep your powder dry.

John Truman Wolfe
March 2012

8
A Greek Tragedy: Pulling Back the Curtain on Bankers Gone Wild

Introduction

Twenty thousand battle-hardened troops and cavalry stormed off of 600 Persian war ships onto the Plains of Marathon 26 miles north of Athens.

These were the shock troops of the Persian army, warriors that had built the Persian Empire into the most powerful military presence in the world of 490 BC.

The Greeks were absurdly outnumbered and some of the Greek generals hesitated going into battle, considering that a wait for reinforcements would be more prudent. But one of the generals, Miltiades, counseled attack.

The vote was split, so Miltiades went to the Polemarch of Athens (a dignitary, who by custom was permitted to vote with the generals). His name was Callimachus.

The Greek historian Herodotus, the "Father of History," reports the conversation between Miltiades and Callimachus.

"With you it rests, Callimachus, either to bring Athens to slavery, or, by securing her freedom, to be remembered by all future generations."

The Greeks attacked. They fought for their lives. They fought for their families. But most of all, they fought for their freedom.

When it was over, 6400 Persians lay slain on the field of battle. One hundred ninety-two Greeks had died.

The Battle of Marathon was the first of the three battles of the Persian Wars between Greece and Persia — the outcome of which would alter the course of Western Civilization forever.

(According to legend, it was a man named Phidippides, who ran the 26 miles from Marathon back to Athens in three hours to tell the Athenians of the great victory. He died after delivering his message. It is the modern day marathon that memorializes his run.)

It was the victory at Marathon, and subsequent victories over the Persians, that created the sense of pride and power that ushered in the century of Athenian greatness known as The Golden Age of Greece.

During these years, Greece produced: one of the greatest statesmen in human history — Pericles; two of the most preeminent thinkers the world has ever known, Socrates and Plato, who brought whole new realms of thought and philosophy to the Western World; the Parthenon, which is still revered as one of the architectural marvels of the world; and a culture imbued with a majesty in art, literature, and theater.

Greece is the birthmother of Democracy.

Today, the former Athenian nation-state, takes the spotlight as the lead in a pitiful play, which shines the spotlight of history on that nation's economic chaos. The play is produced by the International Monetary Fund and is directed by perennial banking bad boy, Goldman Sachs. It is titled, *The Global Financial Crisis.*

I know it is a harsh metaphor, but the Glory that was Greece is gone. That was then and this is now, and the country has become a broken pawn in a real life drama that is being played on the stage of international finance. Some of the cast know it is a play. Most do not. The audience — legislators, regulators, finance ministers, and nations large and small — think it is real. Which it is.

They just don't know that it is an orchestrated reality. Here's the story.

Debt as Addiction

The political descendents of those magnificent Athenians are addicts today. Like a junkie on Horse, they are driven by an insatiable lust to spend. And like all governments, they spend without regard to consequence — on war and welfare, on interest and infrastructure, on beggars and banks, on anything that will keep them in power and soothe their collective Marxian conscience.

To feed their habit, they must borrow.

The Greeks have borrowed in excess of $330 billion. This is a meaningful sum anywhere. In Greece, it is Everest.

The Greek Tragedy has been shoved off of the front pages of the financial press by their Euro-cousins in Ireland as this is written. And Ireland will soon be followed by Portugal and Spain. Still, I am using Greece for illustrative purposes because this kind of financial freebasing has turned the planet into a playground for the ultimate drug dealers — the pirates in pinstripes. It is time it was exposed and hung from the yardarm of public opinion.

Here's how that rolls out.

The Greek economy is managed like a free drug clinic in the Haight Ashbury. The government provides literally hundreds of benefits and subsidies: health care is essentially "free," civil servants can retire with pensions in their 40s, and the government run utilities and enterprises lose more money than a convention of Bernie Madoff investors. Greek legislators must have apprenticed with the financial masterminds in the United States Congress: the Post Office is broke, Am Track is broke, Social Security is broke, Medicare is broke, Fannie Mae and Freddie Mac are broke, and AIG, the insurance company that the government acquired last year, has cost the taxpayers $182 billion... so far.

In 2001, Greece wanted to get into the European Union (EU). They also wanted to use the Euro as their national currency (The countries in the EU that also use the Euro are referred to as the Eurozone. Not all European Union members use the Euro.)

But their debt was too high. Too much welfare, too many pensions, too much interest and the 12th largest military budget in the world (taken as a percentage of GDP). Perhaps they are still fighting the Persians in their collective mind.

In any case, the EU said, "No can do."

What to do?

Some suggested that the country cut back on spending and use their income to pay their debt down. But these people were arrested and burned at the stake as economic heretics.

The problem seemed unsolvable to the money men of Athens. How do we get into the European Union with our current debt load? How do we get in, and also keep the needle in our veins?

In the distance we hear a bugle signaling a cavalry charge. This is followed by the sound of screeching tires as a Humvee stretch-limo the size of *Hindenburg* squeals around the corner, roars up the street and pulls to a stop in front of the Presidential mansion in Athens.

The chauffeur exits the driver's side and walks briskly around the car and opens the rear door. The first person out is a Julia Roberts look-alike in a *Valentino* pantsuit. She is wearing designer shades and is carrying a Prada briefcase. She is followed by an unusually tall man wearing a midnight blue Armani suit with teal pinstripes. He is ostrich egg bald, is wearing granny glasses and has a

Tumi laptop bag slung over his shoulder. He is furiously working the keys of a Blackberry while talking on a Bluetooth headset.

Goldman Sachs has arrived.

Greek treasury officials fall to their knees and weep with joy.

Saviors of nations, bankers to the over-borrowed, Goldman is there to help. Help, that is, as long as the country is willing to pledge some national assets with their tax revenues attached as collateral. They are team players, by God; give them some of your country's tax revenue and the boys from Goldman Sachs will climb any mountain, ford any stream, follow any rainbow till you find your dream (a lender with deep pockets and the ethics of a crack dealer).

What that dream looked like in real life was a package of financial sophistry that camouflaged Greece's debt, pushed it onto the backs of their children, got them into the EU and enabled them to continue to feed their habit.

A "fix" by any other name...

In short, Goldman converted ten billion dollars of Greek debt that had been purchased with U.S. dollars and Japanese yen into debt that could be repaid in Euros. However, in creating this "currency swap", they used a fictitious value for the Euros which lowered the reported amount of Greek debt by billions.

The structure enabled Greece to owe billions to Goldman in a currency deal without having to report it to the

European Union as a loan, which is clearly what it was. Turns out using the Alice in Wonderland value for the Euro wasn't illegal, just deceptive as hell.

Having cut the deal, Goldman's covert loan needed to be paid. Greed never sleeps. And since the faux currency swap was not officially a loan, Goldman had to have some way to get repaid other than "loan payments". To wit, the pirates of pinstripe go on a Hellenic treasure hunt and wind up commandeering the rights to a few of the country's income producing crown jewels — airport fees, the national lottery and toll road income.

Pericles, where are you?

Securing the rights to the tax revenues, they wrap the repayment into an interest rate swap. (Don't go to sleep on me now, I'll explain).

Greece had previously issued some bonds and had to pay the bond holders a fixed rate of interest of 4%. So, as their part of the swap, Goldman agreed to pay Greece a fixed rate of 4%. In return, the government of Greece agreed to pay Goldman a floating rate.

The exact amount Greece had to pay Goldman is not known. However, what is reported is that Goldman received a rate in excess of LIBOR (the rate set in the UK that banks charge each other for short term loans) + 6.6%.

The rate was floating, not fixed, but note that even if LIBOR was zero — 0% - (which it wasn't) Goldman would be paying Greece 4% but would be receiving

6.6%. The absolute worst they could get, then, was an annual profit of 2.6% on a deal for $10 billion in bonds ($260,000,000).

But that's not really enough to push those year ending Goldman bonus babies to the Hamptons. Oh no, not by a long shot, because Goldman also picked up a fee to arrange this charade of about $300,000,000.

In summary, Goldman arranges what appears to be a currency swap for Greece, which is really a loan that doesn't have to be reported to the EU as such.

In so doing, Greece pushes its existing debt back to the future, is accepted into the European Union, gets yet another loan, and still has access to the debt needle.

Goldman gets a fee of $300,000,000 for setting the deal up and ongoing revenue from an interest rate swap estimated at $260,000,000 a year from government owned assets.

Yeah, Baby!

Of course, the story doesn't end there. But then you knew that, didn't you?

Enter The National Bank of Greece

In 2005, Goldman apparently, and we say, "apparently" as all of these figures are a matter of news reports, not official Goldman records, having received their eye watering fee and having recouped about a billion dollars from the interest rate swap (which is what they were reportedly out of pocket on the deal), sold the balance of the deal to the National Bank of Greece.

At this point, Goldman is out of it; Greece has joined the European Union and it now owes the balance of the off balance sheet loan of about $9 billion to their homies at the National Bank of Greece.

All is well...well, that is until 2008 and the eruption of the Global Financial Crisis.

The Hellenic Swap

As the planet's financial system started to go into the DTs, the European Central Bank did what all central banks do at such times, they went to print mode. They structured a program designed to pour billions of Euros into the European banking system.

The National Bank of Greece wanted some of that cheap coin. They could borrow it from the European Central Bank (ECB) and lend it out at handsomely higher rates. Yum, yum. But to get it, they had to pledge some collateral to the ECB, collateral they didn't have.

What they did have was the income stream from the government tax revenues that they had purchased from Goldman three years earlier. There was just one problem, the European Central Bank would not lend to them on that deal. They needed to pledge some bonds.

It's midnight in Athens. From the roof of the head-quarters office of the National Bank of Greece we see a gigantic spot light beaming an enormous image of a dollar sign into the Mediterranean sky, a la the Bat Signal.

The next morning, the Humvee is back with Julia, baldy and their Blackberries. Goldman goes into closed-door session with representatives of the National Bank of Greece and the Treasury officials of the Hellenic Republic. At this point, the Greek government owes the National Bank of Greece about seven billion dollars.

Goldman channels Houdini yet again. They create and execute what has come to be called "The Hellenic Swap." And if you want to see some sleight of hand on the stage of international finance, watch this, because this kind of fiscal alchemy is going on 24/7 around the planet with governments large and small.

In December, 2008, Goldman arranges an interest rate swap between the Greek government and the National Bank of Greece (The Hellenic Swap).

Under the terms of this arrangement, the Greek Government (the Hellenic Republic) is to receive fixed interest payments from the National Bank of Greece of 4.5 % on $6.96 billion dollars.

In return, Greece agrees to pay the National Bank of Greece an interest rate of LIBOR + 6.6% on that amount of money. LIBOR was .8% at the time, making the Greece's interest rate 7.4%. This rate could fluctuate but could never go below 6.6%

As can be seen, the National Bank of Greece makes a profit of 2.9% on this swap (about $201,000,000 a year). Nice. Except the National Bank of Greece doesn't keep the swap. Not exactly.

Shortly after setting up the interest rate swap between the government and the bank, Goldman sets up an entity in London called Titlos, PLC. The name isn't important, but what they do is. Titlos is what is called a "Special Purpose Vehicle (SPV)." That means it is a legal entity that was set up for the sole purpose for conducting a financial transaction.

Titlos issues $6.96 billion worth of notes on which interest is payable.

Titlos then trades the notes to the National Bank of Greece in exchange for their rights to the Hellenic Swap.

It so happens that the notes issued by Titlos are the same
amount as the balance of the loan that Greece owed the
bank ($6.96 billion).

Greece now owes **Titlos** the $6.96 billion and is paying
the Goldman created shell the 7.4% interest while receiving
a fixed rate of 4.5%.

Titlos receives money, takes an administrative fee and
the 4.5% that it must pay Greece, and pays the balance
to the National Bank of Greece which services the interest
due on the notes.

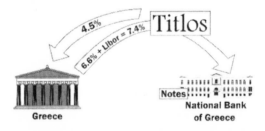

And Shazam! The National Bank of Greece now has
bonds that it can pledge to the European Central Bank
so they can borrow some of that cheap money and lend
it dear. In essence, Goldman has become a Central Bank
creating money out of thin air.

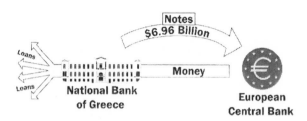

We love you, Goldman.

(Two years later, when the country is on the verge of financial collapse, Goldman issues a statement downgrading the National Bank of Greece saying, "Greece faces both a liquidity and, potentially, a solvency problem. While we believe that, individually, Greek banks tend to be well-run, the problems they face are outside their operational control.")

Isn't that sweet?

The Greek Bankruptcy

Meanwhile, the Athenian addiction continued.

The country finally hit the wall about a year ago, at which point there was a real potential that the nation of Pericles was going to declare bankruptcy.

What does this mean? It means that Greece had reached the point that they could no longer pay the interest on their debt — their bonds.

Markets roiled as Greece went cap in hand to their brethren in the European Union, "Buddy, can you spare a billion?" The Eurozone countries bitched, protested, and criticized, and in the end, along with help from the IMF, coughed up $146 billion.

It wasn't altruism, mind you. No, no. This was pure self interest. The situation in Greece had helped to drive the value of the Euro down 15% during the first six months of the year. (George Soros, the Dorian Gray of international finance, must have been orgasmic). The bailout halted the fall.

If Greece had gone bankrupt, the Euro would have become a door mat on international currency markets and Eurozone economies would have descended into some kind of fiscal horror show.

But it wasn't just the sky-diving currency that got them to pony up: European banks including those in France, Germany, and Switzerland held over $200 billion dollars worth of Greek debt. Just like their good ole' Uncle Sam, with banks at risk, Greece became "too big to fail."

The Greek Tragedy Goes Global

The deeper problem is this: it isn't just Greece. In what can only be described as one of the world's more disgusting acronyms, Spain, Ireland, and Portugal have now been included in the fraternity of the financially fallen, which is referred to in the financial press as the PIGS

(Portugal, Ireland, Greece, and Spain). Italy is often included which expands it into PIIGS. Some include Great Britain, which makes it PIIGGS. Still, a pig by any other name....

The following lead from the May 6, 2010 issue of *World Politics Review* is one of countless articles exposing the fact that the deficit ridden PIIGS could bring down the economies of Europe.

> *With last year's swine flu scare already a distant memory, the risk of a new epidemic is spreading across Europe. This time the fears have to do not with the H1N1 virus, but with the debt contagion facing Europe's PIIGS: Portugal, Ireland, Italy, Greece and Spain. With each of these countries carrying high debt-to-GDP ratios, financial markets are growing increasingly skeptical that Greece's debt crisis will be successfully quarantined within its borders.*

No surprise really when one considers that 15 of the 16 zone members have used swaps to "manage" their debt.

A UPI story of November 13, 2010 states,

> *"The BBC said Irish officials were holding preliminary discussions with the EU about getting assistance from the European Financial Stability Fund. Officials estimated the country would need a bailout of $82 billion to $110 billion."*

Irish officials denied that they were seeking a bailout until the EU agreed to cough up $115 billion on November 29th so that Ireland could follow in the footsteps of their Hellenic brethren — the debt needle inserted deeply in the fiscal vein while the country goes slowly unconscious.

IMF, drug dealers to the world.

The point here is not Ireland, or Greece, for that matter.

Greece was representative of a larger problem in the PIIGGS. But the problem in the PIIGGS is representative of the entire planet — a world mired in a vast interconnected Ponzi scheme of more than a $1.1 Quadrillion dollars of derivatives, $600 trillion of which are interest rate swaps — a scheme that is so vast, even the people who built it have lost control.

American banking is not immune. U.S. banks have $216 trillion in derivatives: JPMorgan $81 trillion, Bank of America $38 trillion, Citibank $29 trillion, Goldman Sachs $39 trillion, HSBC North America $3.4 trillion, Wells Fargo $1.8 trillion; this according to the Office of the Controller of Currency's quarterly report for the first quarter of 2010 and the March 30, 2009 article *Geithner's Dirty Little Secret* by William Engdahl). Historically, 60% of derivatives are interest rate swaps. Do the math.

(Note: the derivatives market consists, to large degree, of bets on other people's bets. A swap is made [which is really a bet on which way interest rates will go, or whether a country's bonds will be repaid, etc.] and then other people and institutions bet on which way the swap will go, and then others bet on that bet and others bet on.... In short, it's a colossal ponzi scheme operating as a global casino, built on hot air and greed. So, lots of people are betting a derivative will go one way and a corresponding number are betting the opposite. If all of these bets were called at the same time, many would cancel each other out. If all of the bets on bets are washed out, the actual money at risk is about 20% of the face value of the derivatives market. Still, we are talking about trillions.)

Which brings us back to what is truly driving the actions of the Fed, the International Monetary Fund and the Bank for International Settlements.

Perhaps you have noticed that the Federal Reserve (which we remind you, is owned by the major New York banks, not the U.S. government) has kept interest rates at zero for the last two years.

What happens to the banks who bet on low interest rates using interest rate swaps? They made billions in profit. Why? Because they arranged to receive fixed rates from borrowers (cities, states, universities) in exchange for floating rates. The floating rates were tied to the Federal Reserve's Fed Funds rate, which was lowered to zero due to the "financial crisis."

Consider the fact that the financial crisis seems to have missed JPMorgan, who made about $5 billion in profit on interest rate swaps during the first 9 months of 2008, the very heart of the crisis.

Goldman Sachs made similar profits on these swaps as did Wells Fargo, to name a few. Of course, the cities, counties and states that took the other side of these bets on the advice of investment bankers to protect their bonds, got slaughtered. But let's not be too harsh on them. According to Goldman Sachs' CEO, Lloyd Blankfein, following his testimony before Congress, he's just a banker "doing God's work."

We love you, Lloyd.

But here's the problem.

The majority of the more than half a quadrillion dollars in interest rate swaps are **held mainly by banks.**

Stay with me here.

With rates at zero, what's the only way they can go?

That's right, up.

And what will happen to those banks with trillions of dollars of interest rate swaps in their portfolios when rates start to climb?

The planet is drowning in a multi-trillion dollar game of banker baccarat, whose players will suffer massive losses when rates reverse.

Will the Fed warn Goldman and JPMorgan about a coming increase in rates so that they can dump their swaps on some other drunk in the casino? Perhaps, but to whom do you sell trillions of dollars of hot air after someone has stuck a pin in the balloon?

And at this point, this isn't entirely up to the Bennie and the Jets. The U.S. Government went $1.4 trillion in debt last year and recorded a $1.3 trillion deficit this year.

Which means?

Which means that for China, Japan, or the tooth fairy to buy our Treasury Bills now, rates will have to rise. China is not drinking Tim Geithner's Kool Aid. And the U.S. government will have to raise rates at some point to entice others to buy our fiscal waste. If we don't raise them, the market will force them up.

Not, says Ben, on my watch. The bald one just announced he was going to buy $600 billion dollars worth of U.S. government debt starting immediately. Ben calls the Alice in Wonderland money injection, "Quantitative Easing." This is the second round of quantitative easing-the first one was an unqualified disaster — so this one is now referred to as QE2.

Sounds like a Steven Spielberg created alien robot.

Ben is nothing if not brilliant. If he takes to the presses and buys Timmy Geithner's debt he doesn't have to rely on his comrades in the People's Republic of China to buy it. Rates will stay low. And the trillions of dollars of interest rate swaps — which are owned by the same people who own his bank — will be safe.

Ben could be up for a Pulitzer Prize.

Except that's not what happened. Finance ministers from around world issued statements implying that Ben was smoking something. And as noted by Mike Larson, of *Money and Markets,* some of the key U.S. government bond yields not only didn't go down, they soared.

And what did our bankers, the Chinese, do? The Chinese credit rating agency, Dagong Global, downgraded the debt of the United States citing, "...the detrimental effects of the QE2 plan and the U.S.'s sizable debt load."

Oops.

A final thought.

What if, just what if, monetary systems were based strictly on products and real estate values.

Currency would not be paper, based on government dictate, and it wouldn't be based on gold (though a gold based currency would be better than fiat, the price of gold can be manipulated.)

The money in circulation would represent the goods and services available to be purchased. There would be sufficient money to buy what was available to be bought. The more productive a country, the more money it would have.

You couldn't pull a Federal Reserve prank and inflate the currency or deflate it for that matter, which is what causes roller-coasting economies.

There are details to work out: It would take an annual survey of actual GDP, and the currency in circulation would have to be adjusted annually to correspond with actual products. But think about it: a monetary system based on actual products.

Meanwhile, keep your powder dry.

9

The Financial Crisis:
Act Three

It would have been Shakespeare's greatest tragedy…and farce…and drama.

It is a play of such power that it brings sovereign nations to their knees and sends Presidents and Prime Ministers to the dustbin of history.

But Willie Shakespeare didn't write this play. It was penned by bankers of Mordor, better known as the Bank for International Settlements.

It was they who took quill in hand to script this drama. They also Executive Produced the play and brought in the bad boy of international finance – the International Monetary Fund (IMF) – to direct.

Headquarters of the Bank for International Settlements in Basel, Switzerland.

Entitled "The Global Financial Crisis," Act I opened on Wall Street with a 778 point drop in the Dow in September of 2008 and was followed by a command performance in the U.S. Congress shortly thereafter. I examined Act I in great detail in *Crisis by Design The Untold Story of the Global Financial Coup* (www.crisisbydesign.net).

Act II, sub-titled *The European Financial Crisis*, is currently being performed daily in the streets of the PIIGS (Portugal, Italy, Ireland, Greece, and Spain) for standing room only audiences in the respective parliaments (see my essay, *A Greek Tragedy: Pulling Back the Curtain on Bankers Gone Wild*, http://johntrumanwolfe.com/products-page/).

There is a theme to this play – a message really. The message, subtle at first, now roars from the pages of the financial press like a raging forest fire demanding solutions that have, in fact, been long since preordained: the crisis is too overwhelming for any one country to deal with; sovereign nations can no longer manage their own financial affairs – international financial organizations – the IMF – must act to save these economies.

If society is going to be saved from a caldron of financial chaos, loans must be made to the governments affected by the crisis as well as to the banks in their countries that are *too big to fail*. (It is these very banks, of course, that buy the government debt and thereby keep the fiscal needle in the arm of those in power).

These people have the IQ of roadkill – the countries are in financial crisis because they borrowed too much. The IMF's solution is to lend them more money.

Hellooo?

But they are not really "stupid" in that sense. Oh no. They know exactly what they are doing. The junkie is hooked.

The banker keeps the needle in the vein, because without it... society goes into withdrawal. And like the agony and convulsions of a body coming off of smack, countries with dependent populations that are forced to live within their means, experience civil unrest, riots, and political chaos.

Withdrawal by any other name....

Politician become nauseous, and retch endlessly behind closed doors considering such things.

They posture for the press, and speak of national sovereignty and fiscal austerity; but in the dark paneled rooms where they once held power, they beg for bail-outs in disgustingly propitious tones.

The money comes... as long as the government signs the loan agreement that comes with it, giving de facto control of their financial, and other governmental, affairs to the IMF, who, in turn, serve the poppy growers in Basel.

Planet Earth Finance for Thee and Me

Governments are addicted to spending. The addict metaphor is apt. They are hooked. Welfare, War, Interest on their debt – they spend and spend and then they spend some more, and always more than they collect in taxes and other fees.

To make up the difference between what they spend and what they rake in from the public, they borrow. They do this by issuing IOUs called bonds. The bonds pay interest to those that buy them.

According to the *very best people*, it is a mortal sin for a country not to honor the interest on its bonds. Worse than that, if they default, they won't be able to borrow again. Remember, they're addicts.

The central banks, commercial banks and other countries buy the bonds. And everyone lives happily ever after.

Eh… well not quite, because at some point, the bonds must be repaid. Governments repay the bonds, of course, with their revenues….Just kidding. They "roll over" the old debt by selling new bonds to repay those that are maturing.

And since these geniuses (who pass laws about accounting and consumer financial protection) always spend more than the government receives, they not only sell new bonds to pay the old ones, they also issue new debt to cover the current shortfall (the U.S. budget short fall **this year**, is a mind bending $1.3 trillion.)

They are members of The Church of the Holy Beltway and it is a violation of their religious faith to cut government spending. Those that advocate reduced funding for war or welfare are crucified on the cross of CNN (for welfare) and Fox (for war) and then, if still breathing, are excommunicated from the church and expelled from the Beltway. So they borrow more, and the debt soars like a space shot out of Cape Canaveral.

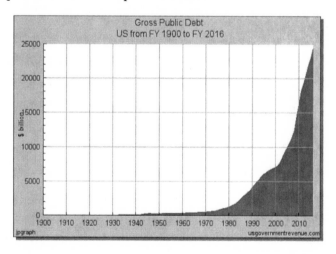

This kind of operation is known as a Ponzi scheme.

It is this kind of operation that put Bernie Madoff in the Federal Pen.

The international bankers (IMF, World Bank and – behind the scenes – the Bank for International Settlements) know this scenario. They sit like vultures in their apocalyptic penthouses waiting for the country to gush so much red ink that they can't even pay the interest on their loans. And then they drop in with a sympathetic smile, a tsk-tsk, and a loan that will cover the interest due to their lenders. Of course the loan comes with just a few conditions, including a loan agreement drafted by the ghouls of the New World Order.

But I am getting ahead of myself. Because it is the central banks of the respective countries that insert the first needle in the vein; they buy their government's debt or see to its purchase.

They print up enough to cover the ongoing shortfall and "lend" it to the government. This goes on and on and on until the government is so bloated with debt, that they can't cover their interest payments, at which point, International bankers push the media button and swoop in for the kill. That is what is going on in Europe right now – the IMF is in swooping mode.

But not all central banks are created equal. No, no. The U.S. Federal Reserve Bank is the Jabba the Hutt of funny money.

It has been the "lender of last resort" not only to the United States government, but the rest of the planet's banking elite as well. As has been covered elsewhere, they come by their dollars the old fashioned way – they make them up out of thin air.

You might wonder what control the U.S. government has over the Fed's ability to create money (U.S. dollars) and Santa Claus it around the planet.

Absolutely none. They can enter a 1 and 12 zeros into a computer, call it a trillion dollars and send it wherever they damn well please.

Due to the efforts of U.S. Congressmen, Ron Paul and Alan Grayson, the first audit of the Federal Reserve in its 100 – year – history was conducted by the Government Accounting Office (GAO). It revealed that Bennie and the Feds made $16 trillion in loans to U.S. and foreign banks during the financial crisis in 2008 and 2009.

Now, 16 trillion is an easy number to write, but to give you some sense of this amount of money, imagine that you are flying in a jet plane at the speed of sound: 760 miles per hour. Imagine that dollar bills are spooling out of the back of the plane at that speed. It would take 224 years for the plane to disperse $16 trillion.

Think about it.

But this was not a problem for Helicopter Ben (so named because of his reference in a speech in 2002 to dropping money from a helicopter to solve deflation).

Truly out of thin air, Bennie clicked a mouse and made trillions of dollars in loans to all the usual suspects. Take a look:

Citigroup: $2.5 trillion ($2,500,000,000,000)

Morgan Stanley: $2.04 trillion ($2,040,000,000,000)

Merrill Lynch: $1.949 trillion ($1,949,000,000,000)

Bank of America: $1.344 trillion ($1,344,000,000,000)

Barclays PLC (United Kingdom): $868 billion
    ($868,000,000,000)

Bear Stearns: $853 billion ($853,000,000,000)

Goldman Sachs: $814 billion ($814,000,000,000)

Royal Bank of Scotland (UK): $541 billion
    ($541,000,000,000)

JPMorgan Chase: $391 billion ($391,000,000,000)

Deutsche Bank (Germany): $354 billion
    ($354,000,000,000)

UBS (Switzerland): $287 billion ($287,000,000,000)

Credit Suisse (Switzerland): $262 billion
    ($262,000,000,000)

Lehman Brothers: $183 billion ($183,000,000,000)

Bank of Scotland (United Kingdom): $181 billion
    ($181,000,000,000)

BNP Paribas (France): $175 billion ($175,000,000,000)

And many more including banks in Belgium

View the 266-page GAO audit of the Federal Reserve (July 21st, 2011):
http://www.scribd.com/doc/60553686/GAO-Fed-Investigation

Source: http://www.gao.gov/products/GAO-11-696

FULL PDF on GAO server:
http://www.gao.gov/new.items/d11696.pdf

Senator Sander's Article:
http://sanders.senate.gov/newsroom/news/?id=9e2a4ea8-6e73-4b...

Your line of credit has disappeared. The limit on your credit cards have been cut, and those you do have often have rates that would make a Mafia Don drool. But Ben dolled out trillions to the world's banking elite and charged them an interest rate of...drum roll, please...zero percent.

Yep.

Zero, zip, nada, nyet.

Thanks, Ben. By the way, the people from *the home* are looking for you.

Sixteen trillion dollars in loans, out of thin air. To banks that rake in billions in profits. No interest.

I have no problem with profit. It's the mother's milk of American business. Love it. But trillions and no interest?

Oh, did we mention that it is the major New York banks (to whom some of the zero percent loans were made) that own the New York Fed?

Ben and his droids are in control of our money and our banking system and we wonder why they are both in shambles.

It is these banks that are buying the debt of the U.S. and European governments. And if they go down... withdrawal, the bends, the riots.

But now, with European governments so buried in debt they can't breath, it is time for Mordor to turn up the heat in Europe. And turn it up so intensely that the

EU governments have to turn to them for bail outs – a euphemism for more loans.

In the planning stage for years, the shaking, sweating, vomiting, governments of the PIIGS must now turn to The Man, the International Monetary Fund.

Why would the IMF make new loans to these governments? Ah, that loan agreement – the assets of a nation, and de facto political control of the government.

Cute. Or not so much.

This is a coup. A global power grab of the planet's finances – and governments.

The Media Flanks Mordor

Here is the media campaign that is flanking the coup and pushing for an "international solution".

On September 22, 2011 the British newspaper, *The Telegraph* blared, "World Bank Chief Zoellick warns 'World in danger zone.'"

The president of the World Bank, Robert Zoellick, (a former Goldman Sachs executive), is quoted in the article warning that the United States, Japan, and Europe threatened to "ravage the world".

Thanks for the heads up, Bob. We love you.

If you understand that this crisis is orchestrated, the role of the controlled media becomes clear. First, they yowl about the depth and danger of the crisis, positioning it like a deadly virus that will spread from country to country and then they call for the doctor. Listen.

The Financial Times of September 26, 2011, "… Greece has to be managed in a way that does not infect others."

The Washington Post, "Europe's Financial Contagion…. The European debt crisis has already spread like a virus from Greece to Ireland and Portugal, and other countries are now at risk: Spain and Italy are probable candidates for financial problems."

Not to be outdone by her mainstream sister to the South, the *New York Times* used almost identical wording in a headline: "The Danger of Contagion From Europe."

However, the media has now pushed the disease metaphor to the side and is carrying the message for what is to come. The message is not subtle.

The Wall Street Journal, September 23, 2011: "World-Wide Distress Rises as Investors See Futility of Governments, Central Banks".

Well, Ollie, if governments and central banks can't handle it, I guess, we'll have to bring in the IMF.

"The IMF," says the *Financial Times of London*, "must stop playing second fiddle in Europe." The article calls for more lending to Italy and Spain and more power to the IMF.

"Put simply, the world has to recognize that the Eurozone's problems are now too big for the Eurozone alone to deal with. The world has a stake in their resolution. And it has an institution that can channel help: the IMF."

The article goes on to say, "The IMF should start taking the lead in managing the crisis rather than playing second fiddle."

This was written by a Finance Professor out of the University of Chicago. And you wonder why Wall Street is filled with bankers "infected" with globalist think.

There is another agenda at play here as well: those feasting on the crash of the Euro.

This too is driven by a media designed to convince those holding them to dump the currency like so many hot tamales (at which time those helping to create the crisis quietly scoop them up. Can you spell George Soros?).

Talk of the Eurozone disbanding and the Euro being discarded as an international currency are planted stories designed to scare investors out of their Euros so others may buy them.

There will be no disbanding of the Eurozone, and no abandonment of the Euro. It won't happen. It doesn't fit the "Trilateral Commission" planetary structure – North America, European Union, Asia – developed by those homies of the New World Order, David Rockefeller and Zbigniew Brzezinski in 1973.

So, where does that leave us?

Overview

Let me summarize and make some suggestions. Some you've heard before, some not.

1. To repeat, but to make sure it is understood: The European Financial Crisis is a staged play. I don't mean that many of those countries aren't buried in the fiscal bat guano of their own making, they are.

The point is that instead of each country handling their own mess, dealing with their own creditors as they can, a look behind the wizard's curtain will reveal that the bankers of Mordor are orchestrating a media campaign. It forwards the message that the financial crisis in Europe is now too big and too complex for any one country to handle and that the International Monetary Fund must be called upon to salvage the situation.

2. Despite all of the dire predictions to the contrary, the European Union will "survive." So will the Euro. The media dance between Nicholas Sarkozy and Andrea Merkel, is so much theater.

It is much easier for the Bad Boys of Basel to control one European Union, than the 27 separate member states. They put too much time, effort, and political coin into forcing it together to let it fracture apart now.

So the EU stays and so does the Euro.

3. Perhaps nothing has been as "globalized" as has international finance. Which means that some of the radioactive

fallout from the European Financial Crisis will settle here in the US. Here's an example:

U.S. Money Market Mutual Funds are heavily invested in large European banks.

Those banks are awash in the debt of the PIIGS.

So the daisy-chain goes: this little piggy defaults on its bonds; this European bank has to write off those bonds and perhaps some others and it, in turn, cannot pay its loans to the U.S. based mutual funds that have lent them money.

Bear in mind that these are not the money market funds offered by your bank. Those are guaranteed by the FDIC (that is, itself, bankrupt, but has a $500 billion line of credit guaranteed by your Uncle. Your Uncle is sleeping with cousin Ben who can pull money out of a digital hat faster than David Copperfield).

These are large Godzilla-sized mutual funds that have invested the savings of millions of Americans in the debt of European banks (yes, banks borrow, too).

The following chart is from an article at Dailyreckoning.com. (http://dailyreckoning.com/money-market-funds-no-longer-the-worlds-safest-investments/ but appears to have originated at www.agorafinacial.com)

Please govern yourself accordingly. One doesn't curl up on the floor and suck their thumb at such news. One works harder, expands fasters, and also takes steps to

Eurotrash?

The hefty allocation to European debt securities inside America's largest money market funds

Five Largest US Money Market Funds	Fidelity Cash Reserve	Vanguard Reserve Prime	Fidelity Institutional Prime Money Market Portfolio	Fidelity Institutional Money Market Portfolio	BlackRock Liquidity TempFund
Institutional Share Class	FDRXX	VMRXX	FIPXX	FNSXX	TMPXX
Min. Investment Assets	$2,500	$5,000,000	$10,000,000	$10,000,000	$3,000,000
Percentage by Region					
US	30%	52%	38%	26%	35%
Canada	10%	10%	8%	10%	14%
Australia	9%	13%	7%	9%	3%
Japan	6%	1%	3%	6%	7%
Europe	45%	24%	44%	49%	41%

Source: Grant's Interest Rate Observer

WWW.AGORAFINANCIAL.COM

ensure they stand upon the strongest possible foundation from which to create their future.

4. Keep liquid, which means plenty of cash in strong banks. U.S. banks are rated at www.bankrate.com and www.weisssrating.com. These agencies are not perfect as they give you a rating based on a current snap shot, not a trend, but they are much better than guessing. Bankrate.com is free. Weiss charges a modest amount for their reports.

I know interest rates can slide under the belly of a snake these days, but preservation of principal should be your primary concern here.

If you want an in-depth, professional analysis of the strength of your bank or one that you are considering, contact the author.

5. Keep satisfactory amounts in precious metals to hand: 10% -25%, mostly silver.

We have found www.coloradogold.com to have the best pricing and service.

The metals have settled back and have been treading water for the last few months. Silver has even dipped to the $28 range at one point. This has prompted a growing chorus of investment gurus to predict that the bull market in metals is over.

Perhaps they're right. After all, we have been recommending silver as an investment alternative since it was $5 an ounce. It ran up as high as $48 – almost a 10X advance.

But I don't think so. This dog can still hunt. It is currently "play possum".

6. Find an honest and competent real estate broker and acquire some multi-family real estate such as a duplex, four-plex, etc. with a healthy cash flow.Many markets abound with real estate properties that generate handsome cash flow. The rental market will continue to strengthen as the residential housing market continues to deteriorate.

7. Diversify some of your cash – 5%-10% out of U.S. dollars into some other currencies where the country's production and fiscal management are sounder and saner than ours. None are perfect, but the Chinese Yuan, the Norwegian Krone and the Swiss Franc are candidates these days. Everbank in Florida provides deposit accounts in foreign currencies. www.everbank.com.

Or you can do this in an offshore account (see #9 below).

8. If the Global Financial Crisis of 2008-2009 was Act I and the European Financial Crisis now on stage is Act II, will there be an Act III and if so, where will it be?

Yes, and here – the crisis will return to the U.S. for Act III.

This is a prediction. I know this is not up-lifting news, but forewarned is forearmed. And keep in mind that this is no more or no less than an economic intelligence estimate, based on information to hand and an under-standing of the intentions of Mordor.

It is their intention to continue to foster global financial chaos across all selected sectors of the industrialized world, until they have full economic control of the planet.

I know, sounds like a Ludlum thriller, but that *is* their intention.

And I think it is their intention to return the crisis to the United States for Act III. The United States is under their thumb via the Fed, but I think their game plan will eventually involve the IMF taking a more "active" role here. That means more fiscal chaos.

If you understand their intention, you will understand that they will have to inflict enough financial pain – pain that is severe enough – to drive Congress and the country into the arms of Mordor.

I don't know if this will be accomplished or not as there are forces working fervently to prevent this. But whether they succeed or not is not the subject here.

The subject here is what one does financially in order to stay as strong as possible in the face of a hostile economic environment.

9. And in this regard, I suggest moving a respectable amount of your reserve assets offshore and out of U.S. dollars. The alternative currency suggestion from above is 5%-10% in other currencies. But I would move somewhere in the range of 20%-25% of total reserve assets offshore. More if your inclined.

I have previously suggested Panama as a destination for your offshore assets. This was because Panama had some of the strongest investor protection laws in the world, perhaps the strongest.

The operative word is "had." Because they recently folded like a rookie at a Vegas poker table. In negotiations with Timmy Geithner's clowns (US Treasury Department officials) they trashed their world-class bank privacy laws in exchange for a Free Trade Agreement with the US.

The word in Spanish, is almost the same in English: Los idiotas.

Geithner described the agreement as:

"Ushering in a new era of openness and transparency for tax information between the United States and Panama."

You Panamanians had a good 20 years after you threw Noriega out, now you are hooked up with the real hoods.

This is the same Tim Geithner, by the way, now running the IRS, that had owed $34,000 in payroll and social security taxes dating back to 2001 and 2002 when Obama nominated him in 2009.

But the Chinese don't Kowtow to Uncle or cousin Tim, and Hong Kong is the number one offshore jurisdiction in the world. It's a good place to park some assets.

There are at least three reasons to do this:

One is the increasingly perilous condition of the US economy.

Two is Washington's demonstrated inability to deal with the problem in any way other than to make it worse.

Three, moves out of the realm of economics into what I would call *The New American Police State*. The precipitous erosion of civil liberties and personal privacy since 9-11 and, everyone in Washington's favorite war, the "War on Terrorism," is Orwellian in the extreme. The USA Patriot Act eviscerates the 4th amendment to the US Constitution like a gutted salmon. While roving bands of psychologists, called "Behavioral Detection Officers," employed by the oh so Soviet sounding, Department of Homeland Security, now prowl bus stations and sporting events with police dogs looking for "micro-expressions" of anger or disgust or frustration on the face of US citizens under a program code-named, "Viper".

The public moves like cattle now through genital revealing, cancer causing "screening" machines at airports, all in the name of the War on Terror. It is not a science fiction movie, or a metaphorical *1984*, it is the United States of America, 2012.

So moving some assets off shore is a precaution. It's perfectly legal and you need to keep it that way. US citizens must pay tax on income earned anywhere in the world.

You can set up a Hong Kong corporation and bank account in a matter of a few weeks. This is not for everyone. A Hong Kong corporation and bank account run about $2,700 and there are annual accounting and filing fees of $500-$900.

Moreover, there are new reporting requirements from your Uncle that you must file with your tax return.

There are less expensive alternatives in the Caribbean and elsewhere that are about $900 less. But if you are interested in providing some distance and some measure of autonomy between you and the growing American police state, then Hong Kong is the place to go.

It may be that you don't feel that you have sufficient assets to warrant the expense. You'll have to make that determination.

But bear in mind that your IRA can own the shares of the Hong Kong Corporation. That's right, this can be an IRA play.

If you have an IRA, it is either a self-directed IRA (you make the investment decisions, but administrator handles the paperwork) or not.

If you don't have a self-directed IRA, you can convert your existing IRA into a self directed one, or a self-directed IRA can be set up for you from scratch (about $350).

Habor Financial Services of Plano, Texas (Dallas suburb) (www.HFSoffshore.com) handles the liaison with the IRA administrator and can then set up the Hong Kong corporation and bank account, which is owned by the IRA. Kind of cool.

Bullet summary:

Cash. Strong bank.

Precious metals. Mostly silver.

Rental income.

Some foreign currency diversification.

Offshore corporation (In or out of an IRA)
and bank account. Hong Kong.

The Real Solution

These concluding remarks are taken from my book, *Crisis by Design: The Untold Story of the Global Financial Coup* (www.crisisbydesign.net.) But I repeat them here, because if we really want to put a financial system in place that is not controlled by a handful of mad men, then this is the system that would do it.

The real answer is the creation of an international monetary system that is based on property and production. This would have to be insisted upon.

In other words, a monetary system that is not based on fiat money or an unworkable commodity, such as gold, but on what money actually represents, and that is all of the production (goods and services) and property value (real estate and land value) of nations.

For example, a realistic assessment of the country's gross domestic product (GDP) and property value would yield an amount—say $100 billion. The country's national bank would ensure that was the amount of currency in circulation. They couldn't print more or less than that amount, and that would mean no inflation, no deflation, just sufficient money to buy what was available to buy.

This would guarantee that the economy is based on stable and real economic measures. It would be based on the most fundamental definitions of inflation and deflation—inflation being the result of more money than goods, and deflation being more goods than money—and financial matters would be maintained accordingly.

Based on this system each state or country would be allocated, as its money, the exact value of its property, real or personal, as well as its current value of production. The currency would be issued by an international body, which could be the IMF, but only once it is irrevocably and unalterably under the oversight and corrective powers of a legislative body and bound by this monetary system, precluding private, corporate, and political abuse.

In other words, all branches of government would be bound by the formula described above and, thus, neither the executive or legislative branch nor any banking organization could institute policies that are debt based.

Once in place, each year, by careful survey, the extant funds in a country or state would be increased or decreased to match its productivity on the premise that money must exist to purchase that which exists to be purchased.

This would make the pursuit of happiness a reality for all people and make the American dream a global reality.

This would result in actual free trade and resolve balance of payment problems, as the currencies would be interchangeable, all having the same value. Free trade would also include free trade of oil. It would allow for oil exploration that is unfettered by unsustainable monetary policy. It would end currency manipulation and artificial oil scarcity, eliminating the most prevalent cause for current wars, which aside from human death and misery create considerable environmental damage. It would also, obviously, abolish carbon credits. In short, it would create an abundance of energy and a future of productivity in which all life would be able to prosper.

I don't take pleasure or joy in detailing the economic takeover of the planet by a gang of pinstriped hoods. But these are not normal times, and if one is informed, he can take the appropriate steps to protect himself and his family and what assets he may have put away for the proverbial rainy day and for the financial security of himself and his family.

I hope you find these suggestions helpful.

And remember to keep your powder dry.

John Truman Wolfe

About the Author

John Truman Wolfe is the author of award-winning fiction and nonfiction books and articles including "The Financial Crisis: A Look Behind the Wizard's Curtain," "America the Litigious," *Mind Games, The Gift,* and his latest stunning release—*Crisis by Design: The Untold Story of the Global Financial Coup and What You Can Do About It.*

He has been a senior credit officer for two California banks—one in the San Francisco Bay Area, the other in Beverly Hills—and is the co-founder of a prestigious Los Angeles–based business-management company, where, as a registered investment advisor, he oversaw the financial and investment matters of some of the biggest names in Hollywood.

Shortly after the fall of Communism, John made several trips to Moscow giving seminars to leading bankers and senior members of the Russian government. In recognition of his work, government officials commissioned a

208

sculpture of his bust by the noted Russian sculptor Sergei Bychkov, which was placed in the Hall of Heroes of the Ministry of Internal Affairs. Just prior to publication, Chinese government officials flew him to Beijing to consult with them on the causes of and solutions to the global financial crisis. He spent several days in Beijing discussing the information revealed in *Crisis by Design* with these parties as well as doing media interviews for Chinese television.

He has a master's degree with honors from San Jose State University and is the former chairman of the Department of History at John F. Kennedy University.

For more information, please visit:
www.BehindtheWizardsCurtain.com
or www.CrisisbyDesign.net.

ACKNOWLEDGMENTS

To my wife, Barbara, who has been the sounding board for all my writing. She has a wonderful sense of style and has no problem suggesting revisions where she thinks they may be helpful or lavishing praise on the metaphorical morsels that delight her.

The art and science of copy editing (and I think it is both) demands an exquisite understanding of matters of grammar and the elements of style. I am blessed to have as a friend and copy editor Rosemary Delderfield.

With every single project she undertakes, Rosemary applies her remarkable understanding of language and the rules therefor with the skill of the consummate professional. It is like turning your manuscript over to a wizard and knowing magic will occur.

If you write and want world-class copy editing, Rosemary can be reached at rdeld@juno.com.

Thank you goes to the people who helped me fill in the research for this book. Everything I have said in this book is all over the web, but it helps to have people who know how to find it. Karen Walby; Kurt Wilson, the Armchair Survivalist; Mitch Hermann; Alex Serrano, and Jim Criscoe all stepped up and hit it out of the park. Thank you, too, Wendy Bellinger, for doing a last-minute proof as we pushed the book out the door.

Thanks to the creative Kendra for the telling graphic in the Goldman chapter.

A special thanks to Boris Levitsky, whose original vision it was to create a book out of the articles. Without his foresight, this never would have happened.

To Patricia, George, and Nick (the book's designer), whose dedication to publishing this book has exhausted all of the midnight oil in both Colorado and Southern California.

And finally, I'd like to thank Al Gore for inventing the Internet, because it is the ultimate research tool for the writer of nonfiction. I would also like to thank him for inventing global warming and carbon credits as a solution to the problem—not because it will make him billions but because this may turn out to be the biggest con job of all time, and will be the subject of my next article.

Crisis by Design–the Film

Crisis by Design is a feature-length documentary that investigates and reveals the root causes of the worldwide economic crash—past, present, and where it's headed.

An exposé on who's "pulling the strings" and "where the bodies are buried," it explores the gaps between the statements of public figures and their true motives.

Throughout *Crisis by Design* complex economic concepts that baffle many will be explained in a simple, direct format. By the end of the film, viewers will be equipped to reach their own conclusions and both understand and survive the global economic collapse.

The tone is entertaining as well as educational, keeping the audience in suspense until the end, when all of the pieces of the puzzle are assembled for a final reveal.

High production value includes archive footage, dramatic reenactments, and interviews with global experts. As events change daily, a last-minute production window will be kept open to address the impact of late-breaking news stories and how they align with the film's content.

You won't want to miss this high-impact, edge-of-your-seat exposé of the men behind the wizard's curtain who pulled the strings on the global financial crisis.

The film is targeted for release in 2011.

To view the trailer and for more information, visit the website: **www.crisisbydesign.com**.

ENDNOTES

Foreword

[1] "Our Nation's First TRUE Patriots." From Bob Aldrich. Keelynet.com. Web. June 23, 2010.

[2] Richard Rollins. *The Long Journey of Noah Webster*. Philadelphia: U. of Penn. Press, 1988. Print.

Introduction

[3] Stock(s)—Short for stock certificate. A document representing the number of shares of a corporation owned by a shareholder.

[4] Richard Ney. *The Wall Street Gang: The book that tells you how to beat the Wall Street manipulators at their own game!* New York: Avon, 1974. Print.

[5] Ted Warren. *How to Make the Stock Market Make Money for You.* Cutchogue, NY: Buccaneer Books, 1994. Print.

[6] Commodities—A commodity is food, metal, or another fixed physical substance that investors buy or sell. For example, corn, gold, currency such as U.S. dollars and Swiss francs, etc.

[7] See *Confessions of an Economic Hit Man* by John Perkins. New York: Plume, 2004. Print.

[8] Sell short—You think a stock/commodity will go down in price. Your broker allows you to borrow these shares of stock. He then sells them at today's high price. You agree to buy them back at a lower price. When the stock goes down to your preset lower price, you buy them back. You pocket the difference. You lose if the value of the stock goes up.

[9] See "The Crash: Unraveling the Global Financial Crisis: Is the Worst Over?" *Frontline*. August 5, 1997. PBS.org. Web. October 10, 2009.

See also Michel Chussodovsky. "Financial Warfare: How the Biggest Banks Created a Global Crisis." AlbionMonitor.com. October 8, 1998. Web. November 15, 2009.

[10] See "International Financial Crises and the IMF." *Cato Handbook for Congress: Policy Recommendations for the 108th Congress (2003).* Cato.org. Web. November 10, 2009.

[11] New York Fed—New York branch of the Federal Reserve Bank.

1 - The Financial Crisis: A Look Behind the Wizard's Curtain

[12] Subprime—Nonprime or second-chance lending. Borrowers with some late payments or poor credit will get higher interest rates than those for prime borrowers.

[13] Paul Harvey, long-time radio broadcaster for ABC network debuted his radio show *The Rest of the Story* in May 1976, and it continued until his death in February 2009. Wikipedia.org. Wikimedia Foundation, Inc. Web. March 15, 2009.

[14] See Ralph G. Walton, Robert Hudak, and Ruth J. Green-Waite. "Adverse Reactions to Aspartame: Double-Blind Challenge in Patients from a Vulnerable Population." *Biol. Psychiatry* 34, 1993:13–17. Print.

[15] See Steven Holmes. "Fannie Mae Eases Credit to Aid Mortgage Lending." *New York Times.* September 30, 1999. NYTimes.com. Web. November 10, 2008.

[16] See "Important Banking Legislation." *FDIC.gov.* May 15, 2007. Web. November 10, 2008.

[17] Investment banks look over a company and then decide to promote the stock; they do due diligence first, of course, but "underwriting" is more of a sales game than anything.

[18] Securities—Certificates of creditorship or property carrying the right to receive interest or dividend, such as shares or bonds.

[19] See Kathleen Day. "Greenspan Calls for Repeal of GlassSteagall Bank Law." *Washington Post.* November 19, 1987. http:// www.high-beam.com/doc/1P2-1355114.html. Web. November 10,2008.

[20] See F. William Engdahl. "The Financial Tsunami and the Evolving Economic Crisis: Greenspan's Grand Design." January 23, 2008. GlobalResearch.ca. Web. December 1, 2008.

[21] See "Commodities Future Modernization Act of 2000." This act mandated that financial derivatives could be traded over the counter by financial institutions without regulations.

See also James Moore. "A Nation of Village Idiots." Huffington-Post.com. September 18, 2008. Web. September 18, 2008.

[22] See Henry C. K. Liu. "Killer Touch for Market Capitalism." Asia-TimesOnline.com. October 30, 2008. Web. December 1, 2008.

[23] See Liz Moyer and Hannah Clark. "Paulson's Big Leap." Financial Services—*Forbes.* June 1, 2006. Forbes.com. Web. December 1, 2008.

[24] See graphic "The Rescue Plan: The Largest Recipients." *New York Times.* October 13, 2008. NYTimes.com. Web. October 13, 2008.

[25] See Gretchen Morgenson. "Investors in Mortgage-Backed Securities Fail to React to Market Plunge." *New York Times.* February 18, 2007. NYTimes.com. Web. January 15, 2009.

[26] See "Dow Jones Industrial Average Chart." Wikipedia.org. n.d. Web. March 1, 2009.

[27] See "Financial Crisis of 2007–2010." Wikipedia.org. n.d. Web. March 1, 2009.

[28] See Mary Kane."Low Income Borrowers Made Scapegoat amid Crisis." WashingtonIndependent.com. September 30, 2008. Web. December 5, 2008.

[29] See Gordon Rayner. "Global Financial Crisis: Does the World Need a New Banking 'Policeman'?" Telegraph.co.uk. October 8, 2008. Web. October 8, 2008.

[30] See Kenneth Parker. "93% of Mortgages Are Being Paid on Time." *Shelbyville Times-Gazette*. March 6, 2008. www.t-g.com. Web. January 8, 2009.

[31] President Obama to the Joint Chiefs of Staff. www.whitehouse.gov. February 24, 2009. Web. March 1, 2009.

[32] See Tamara Keith. "Some Consumers See Credit Cards Cancelled." National Public Radio. October 10, 2008. NPR.org. Web. December 5, 2008.

[33] Quoted in Edmund Conway. "Call to Relax Basel Banking Rules." Telegraph.co.uk. December 15, 2007. Web. December 15, 2007.

[34] See Jacob Gerber. "Australia's January Manufacturing Index Shrinks for Eight Months." Bloomberg.com. February 1, 2009. Web. March 1, 2009.

See also "Industrial Production Still Falling." *China Trade News*. June 12, 2009. ChinaTradeInformation.net. Web. July 1, 2009.

See also "Japanese Exports Fall by the Most in 7 Years." *New York Times*. November 2, 2008. NYTimes.com. Web. March 1, 2009.

See also Lee Chyen Yee. "Update 2—Taiwan Export Orders Show Asia Slump Deepens." Reuters.com. February 24, 2009. Web. March 1, 2009.
See also "South Korean Exports Fall Sharply." TaipeiTimes.com. December 2, 2008. Web. March 1, 2009.

See also "Recession Tipped as Singapore Exports Fall." ChannelNewsAsia.com. September 17, 2008. Web. March 1, 2009.

See also "Hong Kong's Exports Decline for a 12th Straight Month (Update 2)." Bloomberg.com. November 26, 2009. Web. December 1, 2009.

See also "Export Plunge Leads Record German GDP Drop." IrishTimes.com. February 25, 2009. Web. March 1, 2009.

See also "List of Recessions in the United Kingdom." Wikipedia.org. Web. March 1, 2009.

[35] See Press Release. FederalReserve.gov. October 6, 2008. Web. December 1, 2008.

[36] 401(k)s and IRAs—Savings set aside usually for retirement. Often put into stocks and bonds to allow them to grow in value over the working years.

[37] See Steve Watson. "Former Kissinger Policy Planner, CFR Member Calls for New Global Monetary Authority." Infowars.net. September 26, 2008. Web. November 15, 2009.

[38] See Peter Hartcher. "Obama's Economic Saviour Savaged as Keating Lets Rip." *Sydney Morning Herald.* March 7, 2009. SMH.com. Web. November 15, 2009.

[39] See "World Needs New Bretton Woods, says Brown." AFP.com. October 13, 2008. Web. November 16, 2009.

[40] See M. J. Stephey. "Bretton Woods System." Time.com. October 21, 2008. Web. March 1, 2009.

[41] See Evelyn de Rothschild. Global Financial Crisis. CNBC video. December 10, 2008. www.global-financial-crisis.org. Web. December 12, 2008.

[42] See Dominique Strauss-Kahn. "The IMF and Its Future." International Monetary Fund. Speech at the Banco de España, Madrid, Spain. December 30, 2005. IMF.org. Web. December 12, 2008.

[43] See "After the Meltdown. A Private Roundtable on a New U.S. International Economic Policy." December 22, 2008. AmericanProgress.org. Web. March 12, 2009.

[44] Jaime Caruana is the general manager of the Bank for International Settlements, a post he took April 1, 2009. Prior to that, he was the director of the Monetary and Capital Markets Department of the IMF (July 2006 to April 2009.) Prior to that, he was the governor of the Bank of Spain. The IMF is notorious for stirring

the pot of financial unrest. The Bank of Spain had its finger in the pie of mortgage-backed securities traded as derivatives.

See Jaime Caruana's Biography. BIS.org. n.d. Web. June 15, 2009.

See also "Derivatives Markets in Spain." Ipyme.org. n.d. Web.April 10, 2009.

[45] Gordon Rayner. "Global Financial Crisis: Does the World Need a New Banking 'Policeman'?" Telegraph.co.uk. October 8, 2008. Web. October 8, 2008.

2 - Hitler's Bank Goes Global

[46] G-20—A group of twenty (G-20) finance ministers and central bank governors, established in 1999.

[47] See Jane Macartney. "Compliments, Not Controversy, Mark Hillary Clinton's Beijing Visit." *Times* (London). February 23, 2009. TheTimes.co.uk. Web. April 10, 2009.

[48] See "G20 Leaders Agree on Supervisory Body." ChinaDaily.com. April 3, 2009. Web. April 10, 2009.

See also Natasha Brereton. "FSF Reestablished as FSB, Gets Stronger Mandate." Forex Street. April 2, 2009. FXstreet.com. Web. April 10, 2009.
[49] See Mario Draghi. "Re-establishment of the FSF as the Financial Stability Board." FinancialStabilityBoard.org. April 2, 2009. Web. May 14, 2009.

[50] "Mandate." FinancialStabilityBoard.org. n.d. Web. March 31, 2009.

[51] See Carroll Quigley. *Tragedy and Hope: A History of the World in Our Time.* San Pedro, CA: G. S. G. & Associates, 1975. Print.

See also Charles Higham. *Trading with the Enemy: The NaziAmerican Money Plot 1933–1949.* Lincoln, NE: iUniverse, 2007 (1983). Print.

See also Anthony Sutton. *Wall Street and the Rise of Hitler.* Cutchogue, NY: Buccaneer Books, 1974. Print.

[52] Joan Veon. "Controlling the World's Monetary System: The Bank for International Settlements." NewsWithViews.com. August 26, 2003. Web. March 14, 2009.

[53] Dick Morris. "Ending American Sovereignty." TheBulletin.us. April 6, 2009. Web. May 5, 2009.

[54] See speech by the Honorable Ron Paul, Congressional Record, 111th Congress, page 502. Library of Congress. February 26, 2009. Thomas.loc.gov. Web. April 10, 2009.

"The Federal Reserve has the apparency of being a government entity. While created by the U.S. Congress in 1913, the Federal Reserve is an independent entity headed by a Board of Governors consisting of seven presidential appointees, confirmed by the Senate. And that is where the congressional oversight ends. Although the Federal Reserve has many of the privileges of government agencies, it retains the benefits of being a private organization, including being insulated from Freedom of Information Act requests. The Fed has broad powers including entering into agreements with foreign central banks and foreign governments, but the Government Accountability Office is prohibited from auditing or even seeing these agreements."

[55] See "Interest Expense on the Debt Outstanding." TreasuryDirect.gov. n.d. Web. March 14, 2009.

[56] See Marilyn Barnewall. "What Happened to American Sovereignty at G-20?" April 18, 2009. NewsWithViews.com. Web. April 28, 2009.

"President Obama agreed at the G20 meeting in London to create an international board with authority to intervene in U.S. corporations by dictating executive compensation and approving or disapproving business management decisions. Under the new Financial Stability Board, the United States has only one vote. In other words, the group will be largely controlled by European central bankers."

[57] See Ellen Hodgson Brown, JD. "Big Brother in Basel: BIS Financial Stability Board Undermines National Sovereignty." June 22, 2009. WebofDebt.com. Web. June 30, 2009.

"Article II, Section 2, of the United States Constitution grants power to the President to make treaties only with the 'advice and consent' of two-thirds of the Senate. The Constitution does not expressly provide for any alternative to the Article II treaty procedure. However, historically the President has also made international 'agreements' through congressional-executive agreements that are ratified with only a majority from both houses of Congress, or sole-executive agreements made by the President alone. A congressional-executive agreement can cover only those matters which the Constitution explicitly places within the powers of Congress and the President; while a sole-executive agreement can cover only those matters within the President's authority or matters in which Congress has delegated authority to the President. A sole-executive agreement can be negotiated and entered into only through the President's authority (1) in foreign policy, (2) as commander-in-chief of the armed forces, (3) from a prior act of Congress, or (4) from a prior treaty. Agreements beyond these competencies must have the approval of Congress (for congressional-executive agreements) or the Senate (for treaties). *If an international commercial accord contains binding 'treaty' commitments, then a two-thirds vote of the Senate may be required.*"
[58] See John C. Yoo. "Laws as Treaties?: The Constitutionality of Congressional-Executive Agreements." University of California. June 1, 2000. eScholarhip.org. Web. April 10, 2009.

3 - The Financial Crisis: The Hidden Beginning

[59] Creditor nation—When a country exports more than it imports, it has a balance of payments surplus. When it imports more than it exports it becomes a debtor nation.

[60] See Thayer Watkins. "The Bubble Economy of Japan." San José State University, Department of Economics. n.d. Sjsu.edu. Web. May 1, 2009.

[61] See Anthony Randazzo, Michael Flynn, and Adam B. Summers. "Avoiding an American 'Lost Decade': Lessons from Japan's Bubble and Recession." Reason Foundation. February 2009. Reason.org. Web. May 1, 2009.

[62] See Patrick S. J. Carmack and Bill Still. *The Money Masters: How International Bankers Gained Control of America.* Ave Maria, FL: Royalty Production Company, 1998.

[63] "Basel Committee: International Convergence of Capital Measurement and Capital Standards (Updated to April 1998)." Bank for International Settlements. July 1988. BIS.org. Web. May 1, 2009.

[64] "Capital Requirements and Bank Behaviour: The Impact of the Basel Accord." Bank for International Settlements. April 1999. BIS.org. Web. May 1, 2009.

[65] See Linda Allen. "The Basel Capital Accords and International Mortgage Markets: A Survey of the Literature." Stern School of Business, New York University. December 2003. NYU.edu. Web. May 5, 2009.

[66] See note 1 above.

[67] See "2nd LD: Nikkei Plunges Nearly 5%, Briefly Drops Below 8,000." The Free Library by Farlex. January 15, 1989. TheFreeLibrary.com. Web. May 5, 2009.

[68] "Buffet Warns on Investment 'Time Bomb.'" British Broadcasting Association. March 4, 2003. BBC.co.uk. Web. May 28, 2009.

[69] See "Credit Default Swaps Explained." EconomicsHelp.org. November 11, 2008. Web. May 28, 2009.

[70] See "Frank Partnoy: Derivative Dangers." National Public Radio. March 25, 2009. NPR.org. Web. May 28, 2009.

[71] See Andy Kessler. "Have We Seen the Last of the Bear Raids?" *Wall Street Journal.* March 26, 2009. WJS.com. Web. May 28, 2009.

4 - The Goldman Connection

[72] Matt Taibbi. "The Great American Bubble Machine." *Rolling Stone*, July 9–23, 2009. Web. August 1, 2009.

See "Taibbi's Takedown of 'Vampire Squid' Goldman Sachs." April 5, 2010. RollingStone.com.

[73] *Wall Street*. Released December 1987 by 20th Century Fox. Directed by Oliver Stone. The Internet Movie Database. n.d. IMDB.com. Web. August 1, 2009.

[74] See Thomas M. Kostigen. "The 10 Most Unethical People in Business." MarketWatch.com. January 15, 2009. Web. January 15, 2009.

[75] See Julie Creswell and Ben White. "The Guys from 'Government Sachs.'" *New York Times*. October 7, 2008. NYTimes.com. Web. July 15, 2009.

[76] Timothy Noah. "Robert Rubin's Free Ride." Slate.com. October 30, 2008. Web. July 15, 2009.

[77] "On the Edge with Max Keiser." Max Keiser Internet financial program. July 3, 2009. MaxKeiser.com. Web. August 6, 2009.

[78] See "Barack Obama: Top Contributors." Center for Responsive Politics. July 13, 2009. OpenSecrets.org. Web. August 1, 2009.

[79] David Lawder. "Paulson Sees Subprime Woes Contained." Reuters.com. August 1, 2007. Web. February 1, 2009.

[80] See Randall Mikkelsen. "Banks Sound but Economy to Take Time: Paulson." Reuters.com. July 21, 2008. Web. July 15, 2009.

[81] "FDIC-Insured Institutions Lost $3.7 Billion in the Second Quarter of 2009." FDIC.gov. August 27, 2009. Web. August 27, 2009.

[82] Alison Vekshin. "Bair Says Insurance Fund Could Be Insolvent This Year (Update 1)." Bloomberg.com. March 4, 2009. Web. March 4, 2009.

[83] Fannie Mae, Freddie Mac—Federal National Mortgage Association, Federal Home Loan Mortgage Corporation. Fannie was established in 1938 to turn mortgages into securities to be sold to investors. Fannie dealt in the primary home loan market. Freddie was established in 1970 to compete with Fannie Mae to facilitate the secondary mortgage market. They were government-sponsored enterprises (GSEs); now they are in receivership held by the U.S. Government.

[84] See Alison Vekshin and Dawn Kopecki. "Paulson Plans to Take Control of Fannie, Freddie (Update 1)" Bloomberg.com. September 6, 2008. Web. August 1, 2009.

See also "Transcript for August 10, 2008." *Meet the Press.* August 10, 2008. Msnbc.msn.com. Web. August 1, 2009.

[85] See Erik Holm. "AIG's Bailout Cost US$182.5-Billion." Bloomberg.com. March 23, 2009. Web. March 31, 2009.

[86] See Jim Puzzanghera and Tom Hamburger. "Goldman Sachs Defends $13-Billion Payment from AIG." *Los Angeles Times.* March 21, 2009. LATimes.com. Web. March 21, 2009.

[87] An extrapolation. See Debra Bell. "10 Things You Didn't Know about AIG CEO Edward Liddy." *U.S. News and World Report.* March 18, 2009. Politics.usnews.com. Web. August 1, 2009.

[88] See "Inside the Meltdown." *Frontline.* February 17, 2009. PBS.org. Web. August 3, 2009.

[89] Title 1–Troubled Assets Relief Program, Emergency Economic Stabilization Act of 2008. Pub. L. 110–343. October 3, 2008. Stat. 122.3765.

[90] See John Carney. "Merrill Lynch Paid More Than $3 Billion Bonuses after Suffering $27 Billion in Losses." *Clusterstock.* July 30, 2009. BusinessInsider.com. Web. August 8, 2009.

[91] See Peter Barnes and Joanna Ossinger. "B of A to Get $20B More from TARP, plus Backstop on $118B." FoxBusiness.com. January 16, 2009. Web. August 3, 2009.

[92] See Rick Rothacker. "Wachovia Pays Goldman Millions in Fees." CharlotteObserver.com. November 19, 2008. Web. August 3, 2009.

[93] Excerpt by Matt Taibbi. From *Rolling Stone*, July 9–23, 2009. © 2009 Rolling Stone LLC. All rights reserved. Reprinted by permission.

[94] Andy Borowitz. "Goldman Sachs in Talks to Acquire Treasury Department." HuffingtonPost.com. July 16, 2009. Web. August 8, 2009.

[95] See note 21 above.

[96] See "About Us." WorldBank.org. n.d. Web. August 14, 2009.

[97] See James Bovard. "The World Bank vs. the World Poor." Cato Policy Analysis No. 92. The Cato Institute. September 28, 1987. Cato.org. Web. August 23, 2009.

[98] Sarah Anderson. "The IMF and World Bank's Cosmetic Makeover." *Dollars & Sense magazine*. January/February 2001. DollarsandSense.org. Web. March 15, 2009.

[99] See William McQuillen. "Wolfowitz's New Job Turning Him into Iraq War's Invisible Man." Bloomberg.com. December 7, 2005. Web. August 3, 2009.

Robert McNamara was one of the masterminds, if not the mastermind, behind the Vietnam War. See Thomas Lippman. "'Terribly Wrong' Handling of Vietnam Overshadowed Record of Achievement." WashingtonPost.com. July 7, 2009. Web. August 3, 2009.

5 - Preparing for the Money Meltdown

[100] See "The Debt of the U.S." "The Daily History of the Debt Results." October 2009. TreasuryDirect.gov. Web. October 2, 2009.

[101] See statement from speech "Storms on the Horizon." Remarks by Richard W. Fisher, CEO, Federal Reserve Bank of Dallas, before the

Commonwealth Club of California, San Francisco, California. www.DallasFed.org. May 28, 2008. Web. October 2, 2009.

[102] Do the math. One dollar = 6 in. Two = 1 ft. One trillion dollars = 500 billion ft. 5,280 ft. in one mile = 97,696,969 miles. Speed of sound = 768 mph. One year = 6,727,680 miles. 14.52 years. See Cybe. "What Is a Trillion Dollars?" September 17, 2003. 100777.com, a site for Truthseekers. Web. October 2, 2009.

[103] See Josiah Ryan. "Uncle Sam Will Pay $450 Billion This Year Just to Cover Interest on National Debt." Cybercast News Service. December 16, 2008. CNSNews.com. Web. October 3, 2009.

[104] Pork—Short for pork-barrel politics; where a national politician arm-twists his fellows to get part of the national budget allocated to a pet project back home. For example, a local airport named in honor of the politician built at the cost of millions but which serves ten flights per day, mostly to and from Washington.

[105] See Rick Klein. "Dem Senator: Second Stimulus 'Probably Needed.'" ABCnews.com. July 6, 2009. Web. October 3, 2009.

[106] Das Kapitalian—Das Kapital (1867) by Karl Marx, one of the founders of communism. Developed the idea of political economy as a point of social justice leading to the distribution of wealth.

[107] Edwin Mora. "Barney Frank Says He Knew All Along the Stimulus Money Was Not Going to Be Spent Quickly." CNSNews.com. December 4, 2009. Web. December 9, 2009.

[108] Neil Roland. "Barney Frank: TARP's Comp Curbs Could Be Extended to All Businesses." FinancialWeek.com. February 3, 2009. Web. October 2, 2009.

[109] Elizabeth Howard. "Capitol Offenses." MiddleAmericanNew .com. December 2008. Web. January 15, 2009.

[110] See "Targeting Your 401(k)." *Wall Street Journal.* November 14, 2008. WSJ.com/OpinionJournal. Web. January 15, 2009.

[111] See Matt Moffett. "Argentina Makes Grab for Pensions Amid Crisis." *Wall Street Journal*. October 22, 2008. WSJ.com. Web. October 5, 2009.

[112] See note 10 above.

[113] See Joe Duarte. "Argentina's Pension Grab Sets Dangerous Precedent." Financial Sense Editorials. October 23, 2008. FinancialSense.com. Web. October 5, 2009.

[114] G-7—A group of finance ministers from the seven largest industrialized nations. No developing nations are allowed.

[115] Ambrose Evans-Pritchard. "Argentina Seizes Pension Funds to Pay Debts. Who's Next?" Telegraph.co.uk. October 21, 2008. Web. October 5, 2009.

[116] "Executive Order 6102." U.S. President, Franklin D. Roosevelt. Wikipedia.org. n.d. Web. October 5, 2009.

[117] "Currency Control." Wikipedia.org. n.d. Web. October 5, 2009.

[118] Doug Casey. "The Casey International Speculator." *The Casey Report*. January 2009. www.CaseyResearch.com. Web. January 15, 2009.

6 - The Financial Crisis: What You Can Do About It

[119] Martin Crutsinger. "G-20 Leaders Push Global Economic Reforms Friday." WDTN 2. September 25, 2009. WDTN.com. Web. October 28, 2009.

[120] "Special Drawing Rights (SDRs)." International Monetary Fund. IMF.org. Web. October 28, 2009.

[121] "The CIA Chimes In on Gold Control; Highlights Historical Gold-to-Foreign Holdings Shortfunding." September 26, 2009. BearMarketInvestments.com. Web. October 30, 2009.

[122] See "Gold and the Gold Standard." *MacroHistory and World Report*. n.d. Fsmitha.com. Web. November 1, 2009.

[123] See Nick Barisheff. "August 15, 1971: Inflation Unleashed." Kitco.com. May 5, 2006. Web. November 1, 2009.

[124] Actual recording of President Johnson talking to Robert McNamara. AmericanRadioWorks.publicradio.org. April 30, 1964. Web. November 5, 2009.

[125] See "Gulf of Tonkin Incident." Wikipedia.org. n.d. Web. November 5, 2009.

[126] "Robert McNamara Deceived LBJ on Gulf of Tonkin." RawStory.com. July 8, 2009. Web. November 5, 2009.

[127] Bull market—A financial market in which prices are rising and are expected to keep rising.

[128] St. Louis Adjusted Monetary Base (AMBSL) 1918–2010. Federal Reserve Bank of St. Louis. http://research.stlouisfed.org/fred2/series/AMBSL. Web. November 6, 2009.

[129] See Edward Nelson. "Milton Friedman and U.S. Monetary History: 1961–2006." Research Division. Federal Reserve Bank of St. Louis. *Working Paper Series.* Working Paper 2007-002B. http://research.stlouisfed.org/wp/2007/2007-002.pdf. Web. October 15, 2009.

[130] See Nicoletta Batini and Edward Nelson. "The Lag from Monetary Policy Actions to Inflations: Friedman Revisited." BankofEngland.co.uk. 2001. Web. October 15, 2009.

[131] Spot price—The price that is quoted if you want to buy any commodity today.

[132] See "Deposits." FDIC.gov. n.d. Web. November 6, 2009.

[133] Tom Hundley. *Chicago Tribune.* "Oil Rich Norway Guards Its Wealth." *Seattle Times.* November 20, 2007. Seattle Times.nwsource.com. Web. November 6, 2009.

[134] See note 13 above.

RECEIVED NOV - - 2014

Wolfe, John Truman
Crisis by Design - The
Untold Story of the Global
Financial Coup and What You
Can Do about It

CPSIA information can be obtained at www.ICGtesting.com
Printed in the USA
LVOW11s1314040814

397433LV00001B/258/P